GW01081563

A Learner's Guide to Kaytetye

Compiled by Myfany Turpin

IAD PRESS
Alice Springs

Published in 2000 by
IAD Press
PO Box 2531
Alice Springs NT 0871
Australia
Phone: (08) 8951 1334
Fax: (08) 8952 2527
Email: iadpress@ozemail.com.au

© Institute for Aboriginal Development, 2000

National Library of Australia
Cataloguing-in-Publication data:

Turpin, Myfany, 1972–.
A learner's guide to Kaytetye

Bibliography.
ISBN 1 86465 026 5.

1. Kaytetye language. 2. Kaytetye language - Study and teaching - Foreign speakers. I. Institute for Aboriginal Development (Alice Springs, N.T.). II. Title.

499.15

This book is copyright. Apart from any fair dealing for the purposes of private study, research, criticism or review, as permitted under the Copyright Act, no part may be reproduced by any process without permission. Please forward all enquiries to the Publisher at the address above.

Cover painting by Tommy Thompson and Patsy Ngampeyarte for the Aboriginal Land Commissioner in the Barrow Creek (Kaytetye) Land claim in 1999. In the Altyerre (Dreamtime) the Kaytetye language was born at the Spring at Barrow Creek, Tyempelkere. This painting represents Tyempelkere, the Kwerreympe women and yerreyakwerre (bush onions) which are part of this Dreaming.

Illustrations by Craig Tilmouth, Keith Skinner, Shawn Dobson, Jenny Green, Sue MacLeod

Printed in Australia by Southwood Press

The Institute for Aboriginal Development gratefully acknowledges ATSIC for assistance in funding this project, and for their ongoing support for the Central Australian Dictionaries Program.

Contents

Part one: an introduction to Kaytetye

Part two: pronunciation guide

Part three: the lessons

Preface

A Learner's Guide to Kaytetye aims to give people guidelines about the structure of Kaytetye and how it sounds. The basics of the grammar are explained in a clear way, and linguistic and grammatical jargon are avoided.

However, it must be stressed that this is not a complete description of the grammar. Many aspects of the Kaytetye language are not covered in this publication, and others are simplified to give the learner a good start. The aim is to give learners enough skills to enable them to pursue their own exploration of the language.

Part 1 of *A Learner's Guide to Kaytetye* contains information about Kaytetye and language learning. Part 2 teaches the sounds of Kaytetye and Part 3 teaches some dialogues, grammar and contains exercises. The audio CDs are an essential part of this Learner's Guide.

The CDs

This learner's guide comes with two CDs. As you go through the book you will see symbols like this:

next to any Kaytetye sentence or phrase that appears on the CDs.

The table of CD contents can be found on pages 182 and 183.

Care should be taken in playing these CDs in the presence of Kaytetye people, as images, voices and names of people who have passed away can cause offence.

Acknowledgments

Much of the information and many of the example sentences in this learner's guide are drawn from the Kaytetye to English Dictionary (currently being produced at the Central Australian Dictionaries Program) and the unpublished notes of Gavan Breen, Ken Hale and especially Harold Koch. The work of Janie Ampetyane, Emily Hayes, Alison Ross, Joannie Ross, Tommy Thompson, Margaret Watyale and the many other Kaytetye speakers working on the Kaytetye to English Dictionary is gratefully acknowledged. Without these people, the learner's guide would not have been possible. I am also indebted to Harold Koch, Jenny Green, Angela Harrison and Robert Hoogenraad, who provided valuable comments on the draft of this book.

In putting together *A Learner's Guide to Kaytetye* many ideas and some sections of the text have been drawn from other learner's guides, especially *A Learner's Guide to Eastern and Central Arrernte* (1996) and *A Learner's Guide to Warlpiri* (1996), both published by IAD Press.

* * *

Unlike English, which is spoken by millions of people all over the world, Kaytetye is spoken by only a few hundred people in a relatively small geographic area. The Kaytetye language belongs to the Kaytetye people, and like other Aboriginal languages, it is tied to the land and people to whom it belongs.

Part one: an introduction to Kaytetye

The Kaytetye language and its speakers

It has been estimated that there are about 250 speakers of Kaytetye. The Kaytetye language is one of a group of languages that contains Arrernte, Anmatyerr and Alyawarr, amongst other languages. This group of languages is often referred to as the *Arandic* group, and it has around about 4,500 speakers in total.

Kaytetye is significantly different from the other Arandic languages, and so for example while most Kaytetye speakers can speak another Arandic language, few speakers of other Arandic languages can speak Kaytetye. Because Kaytetye has so few speakers, and is so different from the other Arandic languages, many Kaytetye people are worried that their language isn't getting passed on to younger generations.

Where is Kaytetye spoken?

The heartland of Kaytetye country lies approximately 300 kilometres to the north of Alice Springs. Its border to the south is near Stirling Station and to the north, the Devil's Marbles (Karlwe-karlwe). The main communities where Kaytetye is spoken are Artarre (Neutral Junction), Ilewarr (Stirling), Alekarenge (Ali Curung),

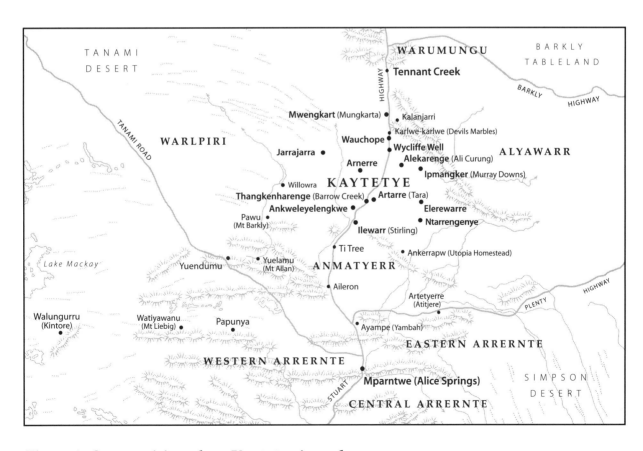

Figure 1. Communities where Kaytetye is spoken

Ankweleyelengkwe outstation, Barrow Creek and Mwengkart (McLaren Creek). There are also some speakers in neighbouring communities, Tennant Creek and in Alice Springs (see map). The neighbouring languages to Kaytetye are Anmatyerr to the south, Alyawarr to the east and north-east, Warlpiri to the west and north-west and Warumungu to the north.

Words from other languages

While there are no dialects of Kaytetye, throughout communities there is some variation as to the vocabulary people use. For example Alekarenge people might use some Warlpiri words, while Stirling people might use some Anmatyerr words and Mwengkart people might use some Alyawarr words. Speakers may even change the words they use depending on what community they are in. For example, while the Kaytetye word for water is **arntwe** many people might prefer to use the word **kwatye** if they are in a community where Arrernte, Alyawarr or Anmatyerr is spoken. **Kwatye** is the word these languages use for water.

Use of English words in Kaytetye

Many English words have been borrowed into Kaytetye and changed to suit the sound patterns of Kaytetye. For example **tyampete** is borrowed from English 'jampot' and means tin or container and the word **wayelethe**, used for radio, comes from the word 'wireless'. It is not uncommon to hear English words spoken in Kaytetye sentences. In this learner's guide we have used an occasional English word in the example sentences, as this reflects the way Kaytetye people speak today. However, some Kaytetye people are concerned that too many words from English and from other Aboriginal languages such as Arrernte are being mixed with Kaytetye, especially by younger people, and that this will eventually lead to the weakening of the language.

Different ways of speaking

There is a noticeable variation between the way older people and younger people speak Kaytetye, characterised by different words, sounds, pronunciation and even grammar. Just as in English there may be different ways of pronouncing a word, there are also different ways of pronouncing some Kaytetye words. You may notice this when listening to the example sentences. For example a word like **apereynenke** 'take' is pronounced more like **apeynenke** by younger speakers. In this learner's guide we have drawn attention to these differences wherever possible. However, remember that just because someone pronounces a word differently, this doesn't mean that it is written differently, so 'take' is always written as **apereynenke**.

Adults talking to babies or young children often use a different way of speaking; their words are shorter and pronunciation different. There are also secret ways of speaking used only by initiated men. The language of ceremonial songs differs considerably from standard Kaytetye. Special words are used to address certain relatives. There is a general practice of avoidance between people related to each other as mother-in-law and son-in-law. These people must avoid each other and communicate through a third person, and even then they use a special way of speaking.

Handsigns and polite ways of communicating

In some situations it is convenient or culturally appropriate to use handsigns rather than speech as a way of communicating, and Kaytetye people are able to have very detailed conversations solely using the complex system of handsigns. There are some situations when a Kaytetye person is not allowed to speak, for example after the death of certain relatives, and in this case handsigns may be relied on completely. Handsigns are also useful for communicating with people who are too far away to hear. For information about handsigns see Kendon (1988). There is also an Aboriginal sign language video dictionary available from AIATSIS in Canberra (the Australian Institute of Aboriginal and Torres Strait Islander Studies).

Different cultures have different ways of showing respect in social situations and greetings and farewells cannot usually be translated easily between languages. For example some English speakers are surprised that in Kaytetye there are no words for 'please', 'thankyou', or 'hello' and 'goodbye'.

Names

Kaytetye people often have several names used in different situations and by different people. They might have a bush name, which is often restricted in its public use, a European first name such as Mary or Bruce, a European surname, a nickname, and a 'skin' name. Personal names are used much less than they are by English speakers, and often people are referred to indirectly as for example 'my brother', 'the one married to Mary', 'that what's-her-name', by references to their country, or simply by using their skin name. It is assumed that everybody would know from the context who is being referred to. Skin names and kinship will be discussed in more detail later on in lesson 3.

It is generally seen as impolite to ask someone their name directly and it is better to find out such information through a third person. In Kaytetye society it is also considered shameful and disrespectful to mention the names of certain kin, particularly mothers-in-law and sons-in-law.

If a person passes away, their personal names (except for their skin name and surname) are not used for a significant amount of time and instead people who have the same name as the deceased are called *Kwementyaye* or they are given another name. The Kwementyaye rule also applies to place names, animals, plants and objects that have the same or similar sound to the name of the person who has passed away— for example, Alice Springs is referred to by some people as Kwementyaye Springs. When someone can't say the name of a place because of a taboo, the word **aheylenge** is used instead of the place name. While use of these terms can depend on how close the speaker is to the deceased, there is also variation between communities and between different generations as to how strictly these cultural rules are applied.

How to use this course

Some features of Kaytetye

Learning a new language is a very exciting thing, and one of the most challenging things for a learner is to discover new ways of viewing the world: seeing through the eyes of another culture and expressing their observations in a very different language.

In order to do this it is important to get an overall feel for the sounds and structure of the new language. Expect to find things about Kaytetye that are different from English, both in the way the language sounds and in the way words are put together in sentences and phrases. Don't always expect to find easy translations between the two languages, as there will be some words in Kaytetye that are very difficult to translate into English and vice versa.

One thing that confuses learners is the way the words are ordered in Kaytetye. Sometimes it seems that this is the opposite of English, or there is no word order at all. The reason for this is that Kaytetye uses endings on words instead of word order to tell such things as 'who did what to whom'. You will learn about this in section 3.5.

Specialisation in vocabulary often reflects to some degree the values and priorities of a culture. On the one hand a single Kaytetye word may cover a range of meanings for which English has different words. For example, **ware** means 'wood', 'fire' or 'heat'; **kwenke** means 'swallow soft food, such as bush plums' or 'insert'; **ngayele** means 'food' and 'hungry' and **arntwe** means both 'rain' and 'water'. At first the connection between these different meanings may not seem obvious, but part of the excitement of learning is trying to understand the logic of the Kaytetye world view.

On the other hand, very often Kaytetye will make a distinction in meaning that is not made in English, as you will discover when you learn Kaytetye pronouns and kin names in section 5.5. For example in English we simply say 'brother' and 'sister' whereas in Kaytetye society there is a distinction made according to whether the sibling (brother or sister) is older or younger. A younger sibling is called **atyerreye**, an elder brother is called **alkereye** and an elder sister is called **arrereye**. Some Kaytetye words, such as **alkaperte** and the Kaytetye skin names, have no English equivalent at all. Try to understand the logic of the Kaytetye world view, and don't assume that it is the same as your own.

The Kaytetye language is very rich in the way it describes family and kin, animal and plant species, the interaction of people with each other and their environment, and the land and its forms. Conversely, there are few number terms—a traditional lifestyle was not oriented towards measurement and numerical calculations. While it is difficult to talk about computer programming in Kaytetye, it must also be said that the language is adapting and incorporating new vocabulary needed to deal with change.

Learning the words and structure of a language is only a beginning towards hearing what is being said. The richness of a language depends very much on the context in which it is being used, and understanding this requires respect and openness towards the culture of the people whose language you are learning.

Structure of the course

In this course you will understand and learn to say many different types of Kaytetye sentences, such as statements, commands, questions and answers. Each of the twelve lessons is structured around a dialogue, and most of the features covered in the lesson are used in the dialogue. It is very important to listen to and practise the dialogue without looking at the written text—playing the dialogue tape in the car or on a walkman is a good idea. Practise the dialogue until you can say it correctly before moving on to the rest of the lesson. The lessons are designed to add one new element—such as an ending—at a time.

Most of the Kaytetye example sentences and words used throughout the course are heard on the CDs which come with this book. This is what they look like:

Nthek-angkwerre nge apenke?
where-through   you go
Where are you going?

You will notice that in the example sentences each Kaytetye word or ending has an English equivalent written underneath. This is called a *gloss*. Some glosses are abbreviations; in this case they are written in CAPS. The glosses aim to help you understand exactly how words and sentences are structured, so that the free translations which are given make more sense. An index of terms specific to language learning is on page 183. These terms are used frequently throughout this course.

The sentences are numbered in both the CD and the book to help you follow with the CD.

At the end of each lesson are some exercises, which are on the CD. These cover the main points learnt in the lesson; however, you will need to do more practice than just the exercises in this book to learn Kaytetye, which is why revising and reviewing are so important. Answers to the exercises can be found in appendix 6.

Also at the end of the book, in appendix 1, there is a theme-based wordlist, a Kaytetye–English wordlist and an English–Kaytetye wordlist. A list of all the endings learnt throughout the course is in appendix 4. Everything on the CDs is also written in the book. You can analyse for yourself what is happening to the structure of the sentences as the new features are added.

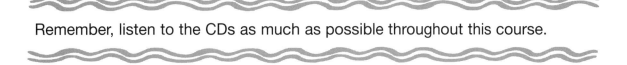

Remember, listen to the CDs as much as possible throughout this course.

Revise and review

It is absolutely essential that you learn each new feature thoroughly before you move on to the next section. You will need to:
- Listen to each new set of sentences, then listen again, repeating them aloud until you can do it with ease.

- Go back and listen carefully for each little piece of the sentence, each word and all the endings to get a feel for how each contributes to the meaning of the sentence. Do this several times and, if necessary, re-read the explanations.
- Go back again, and this time just look at the translation of each sentence and try to formulate it in Kaytetye for yourself, then check if you got it right. Repeat this step until you can do it rapidly without error.

You will then be ready to move on to the next lesson. Keep revising earlier lessons, because that is the basis on which you can add new features. Don't go on until you have all the previous material fluently at your command. This means that working through the learner's guide will take a long time; much longer than just reading through the book and listening to the CDs!

Going beyond this course

You will need to practise Kaytetye regularly in order to go beyond the learner's guide. One way is to attend a Kaytetye language course at IAD. The best way is to talk to Kaytetye speakers where you can use and extend what you know. In order to do that successfully you need to be able to manage the conversations so you aren't flooded with a flurry of Kaytetye coming at you. You need simple but useful things to say, ways to ask questions and give answers that can sustain a conversation. For this reason we include some basic words and phrases for learning Kaytetye throughout the pronunciation guide on pages 8–31. Practise these so you can use them from the start.

If you can't practise with language speakers or in a course you will need some simple techniques to practise and extend yourself on your own. You need to be an active learner to be successful. Here are a few hints:

- Put labels on as many things as you can around the home, office or garden and practise naming them until you can do so without the labels.
- Practise these with endings or simple verbs. For example you could call a fridge **atnwenth-arenge** 'meat place', and **anteyane** 'sitting' could be used in association with a chair.
- Try to read some simple Kaytetye books, such as the set of Kaytetye readers available from the IAD Language Centre, and puzzle out the meaning for yourself. Remember that the English translations may be very free and so may not reflect the exact Kaytetye words.

When you get the opportunity to be around a Kaytetye speaker it is good to remember the following things to help you learn the language:

- Ask for the names of things and practise saying them. Ask people to correct you if you aren't saying them right. Don't be ashamed of not remembering, just keep asking until it is fixed in your mind.
- Keep a notebook in your pocket and write down any new word or expression you hear spoken. Try to work out the meaning.
- Use whatever Kaytetye you have on every possible occasion. Never mind that you cannot say complex things. The trick of learning is to start simple.
- Try to reply to questions in Kaytetye, even if they are asked in English. Remember there is no shame in trying and failing.

If you have a friend learning Kaytetye, you can practise each of the twelve dialogues with them. You can also try making up your own by modifying the dialogues and substituting words.

Key to conventions and symbols used in this book

Hint
These are ways to practise which will help your learning.

Beware
Take care! This indicates that there is a danger of possible confusion.

Note
Important information about grammar, spelling or meaning.

Further information
Interesting background, cultural or advanced information that is not essential to the lesson.

means listen to this example on CD (CD contents are described on pages 182–3).

The examples are numbered like this—**3**—and the numbering starts again at the start of each lesson. Listen to these sentences and repeat them as you go through the learner's guide.

Hyphens (-)
Hyphens are used to join reduplicated words, for example **akely-akelye** (small-small) 'young ones', 'small ones' and before endings of two or more syllables, for example **elpay-angkwerre** 'through the creek'. They are used more frequently in this book than in usual Kaytetye writing, in order to make the structure of complex words more obvious.

Plus signs (+)
Plus signs are used to indicate where endings that are not hyphenated are joined onto words. Thus you can see how the word is made up. For example **nthek-angkwerre ngepe apenke?** 'where are you going' is made up of **nthek-angkwerre nge+pe ape+nke?** In the Kaytetye sentences, pluses are used at the beginning of the learner's guide to help you identify endings. As each of these endings is covered in the lessons, the pluses are dropped and the endings are written straight onto the word.

Square brackets [ ]
Square brackets are used in headings to show grammatical terms.

Part two: pronunciation guide

The Kaytetye spelling system

Many non-Kaytetye speakers are daunted when they first encounter the system used for spelling Kaytetye and other Arandic languages. You may perhaps have noticed the variation in the spelling of Kaytetye words, with even the word Kaytetye itself spelt in quite a few different ways: Kaiditch, Kaitish, Kaytej, Kaidej and Kaytety to mention just a few.

To write Kaytetye, or any other language for that matter, we could use any of the symbols that are used to write down language—for example Arabic, Chinese or Greek characters.

However, most Aboriginal people and other Australians are used to writing English, which uses the Roman alphabet. This is why Aboriginal languages are written with letters chosen from the normal English alphabet, although not all the letters are needed to write in Kaytetye. Kaytetye writing uses the following twelve letters:

A E G H K L M N P R T W Y

Combinations of these letters are used to represent Kaytetye sounds that English doesn't have. **It's important to remember that most of these letters are not pronounced the way they are in English.**

History of the Kaytetye spelling system

Over the last 20 years or so Kaytetye people have worked together with linguists to develop a spelling system that is consistent and reflects the sound system of the Kaytetye language. The spelling in this learner's guide is basically the same as that used in the book *Kaytetye Country* (1993), which is also similar to that used for other Arandic languages—see *Alyawarr to English Dictionary* (1992) and *Eastern and Central Arrernte to English Dictionary* (1994). This is important considering that most people (as well as most schools) use more than one Arandic language. At a spelling workshop in May 1998, people decided to trial various spelling options to ascertain which method would best facilitate learning. Although these decisions still have to be made, we think it's important to get out a book on how to read and write Kaytetye as soon as possible, as there are many people who want to start learning how to read, write and speak Kaytetye.

Several things must be said about the Kaytetye spelling system. Firstly, it is far more logical and consistent than English. The Kaytetye spelling system uses only one letter, or one group of letters to represent one sound, whereas in English many letters and groups of letters are used. For example, in English the vowel sound **oo** which appears in the word 'zoo' is written in lots of ways:

wh**o**	l**ie**u
thr**ough**	z**oo**
t**wo**	l**ew**d
sh**oe**	s**ou**p
bl**ue**	

Similarly, even consonants in English can be spelt lots of ways. Look at the various ways of spelling the sound **n** below.

not   **gn**ome

wi**nn**er   Jo**hn**

knee

Just imagine how difficult it must be to learn the correct way to spell these English words. Fortunately, in Kaytetye it is not so difficult, as one sound is always written with one letter, or group of letters. For example the sound **a**, as in the word **ware**, is always written with the letter **a**.

Another point about the Kaytetye spelling system is that the range and combinations of English letters used to spell Kaytetye words are necessary to describe the range of significant sounds in the language. It is not possible to simply spell things the way they sound in English because the sounds of Kaytetye don't all exist in English. Thirdly, Kaytetye people themselves have had the major input into the design of the spelling system and they have found that this system works well for spelling their language. Once you get used to the system, the Kaytetye language is spelt the way it sounds.

Kaytetye sounds

Every language has a set of important sounds which it uses to make words, and these sounds are called *phonemes*. The phonemes in Kaytetye are very different from the phonemes in English, but because it is useful to make the spelling system as close as possible to English, we use English letters and groups of letters to represent the Kaytetye sounds. A similar spelling system is also used for other Arandic languages, so if you know how to write another Arandic language, such as Arrernte, you'll find learning to read and write Kaytetye is not so different.

Consonants

Kaytetye *consonants* are written with the letters and groups of letters in the table below. The sounds in the table are in the same column if they are pronounced using a similar part of the mouth, such as the lips, tongue, or palate (the labels for each column are the linguistic terms for the part of the mouth used). Sounds are in the same row if they are produced in a similar way, such as by blocking off the mouth so the air goes through the nose, or by letting a small puff of air out after the sound. The labels for each column are the linguistic terms for the way the sounds are made, and they are explained in greater detail in the following pages.

Table 1   Kaytetye consonants

	bilabial	lamino-dental	apico-alveolar	alveolar retroflex	prepalatal	lamino-palatal	velar
stops	p	th	t	rt	yt	ty	k
plain nasals	m	nh	n	rn	yn	ny	ng
pre-stopped nasals	pm	tnh	tn	rtn	ytn	tny	kng
laterals		lh	l	rl	yl	ly	
trills & taps			rr				
approximants	w		r			y	h

All of these consonant sounds have a *rounded* variety as well. They are called rounded because to make these sounds the lips must be round. You can hear rounding in the English **w** sound, as in the words 'window', 'quail' and 'acquaintance'. In Kaytetye this rounding sound is represented by putting a **w** after the consonant, for example:

1   akelye   little (*unrounded* **k**)
     akwelye   rain (*rounded* **k**)

The letter **h** is the only sound which cannot be followed by a **w**.

2   aherre   kangaroo
     awerre   boy, male

If there is another syllable after a rounded consonant, the following vowel sounds like the **oo** in 'cool'. But if a rounded consonant is the last part of the word, then the consonant and vowel sounds like **qua** in the English word 'qualm'.

You will notice that many Kaytetye words begin with **a**, although they may not be pronounced with this **a** all the time. The meaning of the word is not usually affected by including the **a** on the front of the word or leaving it out, though some speakers of the language may prefer to pronounce the word in one way or the other. There are some words that never begin with **a**: for example **mataye** 'cloud', which is never pronounced as **amataye**. There are also a few pairs of words where the **a** at the beginning is the only significant difference between the two words; in this case the **a** is always written:

3	akwerre	coolamon
	kwerre	young girl
4	rtennge	base of skull
	artennge	dirty

akwerre

In any language we tend to leave out some small bits of words when we talk so that there is no sharp break between the words, making speech flow smoothly. For example, people might leave out the **ck** in the phrase 'trick question' rather than saying both the **ck** and the **q**. In Kaytetye the final **e** on words is not heard if the next word starts with a vowel. The only way you can get a feel for this melody and rhythm is by listening to the language and practising speaking.

We will now go through each of the consonants in table 1, starting from the left hand column going down.

Bilabial sounds

The first column has sounds described as *bilabial*. This means that to make these sounds, the top and bottom lips meet, as they do in English.

Sounds spelt with the letter *p*

In Kaytetye there is no distinction between the English sounds **b** and **p**. So sometimes **p** sounds more like **b**, and sometimes it sounds like **p**.

5	pareype	legless lizard
	apeyakele	nothing, no
	apanpe	everywhere

Now listen to **p** when it is followed by **w**

6	pweleke	cow, bullock
	pwenge	old woman, blind

Sounds spelt with the letter **m**

 7
am**am**perle	nice, beautiful
mataye	clouds
mentye	leave alone

There are also words which have another consonant after **m**

 8
wa**mp**ere	possum
pay**mp**elhe	wing, feather

Now listen to **m** when it is followed by **w**

 9
mwekarte	hat
mwernarte	this way
eltye**mw**erneye	policeman

There are also words which have another consonant with **mw**

 10
et**nmw**ernte	shady place where kangaroo sits
mpwerneye	spouse
mpwe	urine

Sounds spelt with the letters **pm**

 11
a**pm**ere	camp, place
a**pm**arleye	uncle
err**pm**alhe	firesaw

wampere

apmere

Further information
errpmalhe is a wooden tool which is rubbed with another stick to make fire.

Hint
The sounds **pm**, **tnh**, **rtn**, **tn**, **ytn**, **tny**, and **kng** are made by blocking the air in the mouth and then letting it flow through the nose. The first sound runs into the nasal sound which follows, making one sound. **pm** sounds a bit like the 'pm' in 'help me'.

Now listen to **pm** when it is followed by **w**

 12
a**pmw**e	snake

Useful expressions 1

perteye?	ready?
alkaperte!	OK, let's go!
me!	here, take this!
yekaye amamperle!	oh, it's lovely!
mentye errpatye	leave it, it's no good

Lamino-dental sounds

These sounds are like English **t**, **n** and **l** except that they are made by touching the back of the upper teeth with the front of the tongue. Note that the tip of the tongue sticks slightly out.

Sounds spelt with the letters *th*

 13

a**th**erre	two
a**th**e	grass
a**th**errke	green grass

Now listen to **th** when it is followed by **w**

 14

e**thw**e	poison
thwetherraye	owlet nightjar

Listen to this word which has another consonant with **thw**

 15

etn**thw**enke	(to) look for

Hint
To learn how to say the **th**, **nh**, and **lh** sounds try this trick. Say 'the' and notice where your tongue is. Now see if you can say 'the' with your tongue in the same position but don't let the air out gradually between your tongue and teeth, instead let the air out all at once, as if you were saying a **d** sound.

Sounds spelt with the letters *nh*

 16

nharte	that
kwerepe**nh**e	after that
atyewe**nh**e	myself

There are also words which have another consonant with **nh**

Note
nh can be followed by **th** but **n** is never followed by **th**. To make this easier to read, the sound **nh** followed by **th** is always written **nth** and never **nhth**.

 17   nthekele   where
         mantharre   death adder
         nthelarte   over there

Beware
Don't confuse **mantharre** 'death adder' with **mantarre** 'clothes'

Now listen to **nth** when it is followed by **w**

 18   anthwerrke   unripe

Sounds spelt with the letters *tnh*

 19   eletnhenke   (to) throw
         atnhakerte   slow, tired
         atnhenke   (to) bite

Hint
Remember the sounds **pm, tnh, rtn, tn, ytn, tny,** and **kng** are made by blocking the air in the mouth and then letting it flow through the nose. The first sound runs into the nasal sound which follows, making one sound.

Now listen to **tnh** when it is followed by **w**

 20   tnhwenge   story heard from someone else

There are also words which have **th** after **tnh**. When writing this combination of sounds (**tnh** + **th**) the middle **h** is dropped so it becomes **tnth**

 21   atnthenke   (to) fall
         aketntheye   plant species (*Eremophila duttonii*)
         etnthwerrane   (to) look for

Sounds spelt with the letters *lh*

 22

elhe	nose
arelhe	woman
lhenpe	armpit

When **lh** is followed by **th**, it is always written **lth**. Listen to this word which has the consonant **th** after **lh**:

 23   althenke   (to) clean, pluck

Now listen to **lh** when it is followed by **w**

 24   alhwenge   hole

alhwenge

 Useful expressions 2

arrernentye?	how many?
atherrarte	two
awenyerr-aperte	only one
apeyakele	none
elpathene nte!	listen!

Apico-alveolar sounds

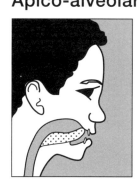

These sounds are the same as the English sounds **t**, **n** and **l**, but only the tip of the tongue touches the upper gums. In these sounds the body of the tongue slouches down to the bottom of the mouth giving the tongue a concave shape, whereas with lamino-palatal sounds the tongue has a convex shape.

Sounds spelt with the letter *t*

 25

atere	scared
etenke	(to) cut
etak-etake	carefully

Now listen to **t** when it is followed by **w**

 26

twerrpe	sandhill
twerarte	all
twatyale	hairstring belt

Sounds spelt with the letter *n*

 27
anenke	(to) sit
anatye	yam
Penangke	(skin name)

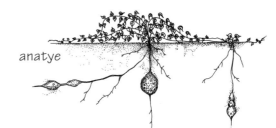
anatye

There are also words which have another consonant after **n**

 28
anteyane	sitting
nte	you
enngerre	face
kwenpe	lower calf
apenke	go

Now listen to **n** when it is followed by **w**

 29
anwengere	outside
enwekele	overnight, camping out
enwenke	(to) lie

Sounds spelt with the letters *tn*

atneme

 30
atneme	yamstick
tneyele	later, next time
atnawerre	straight, correct

Hint
The sounds **pm**, **tnh**, **rtn**, **tn**, **ytn**, **tny**, and **kng** are made by blocking the air in the mouth and then letting it flow through the nose. The **tn** sound in Kaytetye sounds a bit like **t'n** in the word 'eat'n' if you say it with a strong Australian accent.

Further information
atneme 'digging stick' or 'yamstick' is traditionally a Kaytetye woman's most important tool, while men's tools include **errtyarte** 'spear' and **kayle** 'boomerang'.

kayle

There are also words which have another rounded consonant after **tn**

 31
atnke	alive
rlwetnperre	forehead
atnme	red ochre

Now listen to **tn** when it is followed by **w**

 32

atnwerrete	base of kangaroo's tail
atnwenthe	meat
atnwererrke	heel

There are also words which have another consonant with **tnw**. In this case the consonant, such as **k** and **m** in the words below, is written before the **w**

 33

atnkwe	asleep
atnkwarengele	night
etnmwernte	kangaroo shade

Sounds spelt with the letter *l*

 34

aleke	dog
enwekele	overnight, camping out
aney-alpenhe	went back and stayed

There are also words which have another consonant after **l**

 35

| pwelparrenke | (to) swim |
| arralkenke | (to) yawn |

Now listen to **l** when it is followed by **w**

 36

lwethe	half
alwenke	(to) chase
lwemanenke	(to) rise

There are also words which have **kw** following **lw**. In this case the combination of these consonants is written

 37

| alkwarreye | bush banana |
| elkwerre | middle |

alkwarreye

Sounds spelt with the letters *rr*

 38

arrenke	(to) put
akwerre	coolamon
artarre	emu's long tail feathers (also place name)

There are also words which have another consonant after **rr**

 39

arrmaly-arrmalye	soft
errpatye	no good, bad
errpmale	fire saw
akerrthe	antbed
perrtnye	skin

eyte**rr**tye	body, person
ampe**rrng**arrenke	(to) feel sorry for
athe**rr**ke	green grass
a**rrkng**e	blood

Now listen to **rr** when it is followed by **w**

 40

arrwekele	in front
errwenye	feathers
arrwete	beard, whiskers

There are also words which have another rounded consonant with **rrw**

 41

errpwerle	black, dark
errkwere	hot
errtywerne	tooth

 Useful expressions 3

nthakenharrerane?	how does it go? what are you doing?
mpelarte	like that
lwarre?	true?, really?
apenerne nge!	come here!
elper-aperte!	quickly!

Retroflex sounds

 These sounds are written **rt, rl, rn** and **r**. They are made by curling the tongue back so that the underneath of the tongue tip touches the roof of the mouth just behind the gum ridge.

Sounds spelt with the letters *rt*

 42

artenke	(to) chop
artarre	emu's long tail feathers (also place name)
atnhakerte	slow, tired

Now listen to **rt** when it is followed by **w**

 43

artweye	man
ertwe	wet (ground)
artwerrpe	afternoon

Sounds spelt with the letters *rn*

 44
ar**n**e	water vessel
mwe**rn**arte	this way
mpwe**rn**eye	wife, husband, brother-in-law

There are also words which have another consonant after **rn**

 45
ar**n**tenke	(to) break, snap
ar**n**tetye	sick
ar**n**ke	cliff
elpa**rn**kwere	blue-tongue lizard
ar**n**twe	water

elparnkwere

~~~

Note
The **rn** sound does not occur rounded on its own, but it does occur with a **k** or a **t**. So there are no words with **rnw**; however, there are words that have the sounds **rnkw** and **rntw** in them.

~~~

Sounds spelt with the letters *rtn*

artnangke

 46
ar**tn**e	scrub
ar**tn**angke	bilby

There are also words which have another consonant after **rtn**

 47
ar**tn**penke	(to) run
ar**tn**te	stone, money

Now listen to **rtn** when it is followed by **w**

 48
ar**tnw**enge	child
er**tnw**enke	(to) dance (of women)
ar**tnw**ere	dingo

There are also words which have another rounded consonant with **rtnw**. These consonants are always written before the **w**

 49
ar**tntw**enke	(to) tell
er**tntw**enke	(to) push

Sounds spelt with the letters *rl*

 50
ar**l**pe	ashes
Pwe**rl**e	(skin name)
tya**rl**enye	arm

There are also words which have another consonant after **rl**

 51

ar**lt**ere	white
ar**lk**erre	bush tomato
ar**lp**alhe	fur string headband

Now listen to **rl** when it is followed by **w**

 52

er**lw**e	eye
ar**lw**eye	father

There are also words which have another consonant with **rlw**

 53

er**lkw**e	old man
ar**ltw**e	empty
antyar**lkw**e	nest

Sounds spelt with the letter *r*
r in Kaytetye sounds similar to the English **r** in 'red'.

 54

atere	scared
arenke	(to) see
ware	fire

Now listen to **r** when it is followed by **w**

 55

arwengerrpe	turkey
rentyerwenge	brains

arwengerrpe

 Useful expressions 4

elewarte?	when?
rlengkelke	right now
alel-aperte	soon
angkwetye-apertawe	soon!
tneyele arewethawe!	see you later!
ngwenge arewethawe!	see you tomorrow!

Prepalatal sounds
These sounds are made by putting the tongue into the position you would to make the **ee** sound in English, and then make a **t**, **n**, or **l** sound with the tip of the tongue. These sounds are similar to what is heard in the English words '**eat**', '**teen**', '**wheel**', '**plain**' and '**gate**'.

Sounds spelt with the letters **yt**

 56   Kaytetye   (language and tribal name)
           atnyemayte   witchetty grub
           eyterrtye   body, person

Now listen to **yt** when it is followed by **w**

 57   aytwelke   limestone

Sounds spelt with the letters **yn**

 58   areynenge   euro
           aynenke   (to) eat
           apereynenke   (to) take

areynenge

There are also words which have another consonant after **yn**

 59   akeynte   crest of cockatoo
           aynterrke   dry

Note
The **yn** sound does not occur rounded on its own, but it does occur rounded after **t**. So there are no words with **ynw**; however, there are words with **yntw**.

---

 60   ayntwerte   clump of trees

Sounds spelt with the letters **ytn**

 61   eleytne   pigmy monitor
           ahalaytnenke   (to) sing out
           elperlaytnenke (to) whistle

There are also words which have another consonant after **ytn**

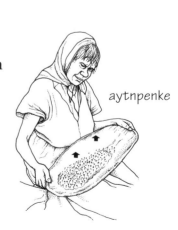

62   aytnmenheye   mother's mother
           aytnpenke   (to) yandy
           eytntenke   (to) smell something

aytnpenke

Sounds spelt with the letters **yl**

63   eylenke   (to) get, pick up
           ayleme   we two
           arreyle   cheek

There are also words which have another consonant after **yl**

 64   aylpele   river red gum
         eylpertenye   wedge-tailed eagle
         eylkelke   ankle bone

Now listen to **yl** when it is followed by **w**

 65   aylwere   young emu

There are also words which have another rounded consonant with **ylw**. This consonant is always written before the **w**

 66   eylkwennge   mouse
         aylpwarele   (to) carry on shoulder
         eylpweralke   sugarbag

 Useful expressions 5

nhante?	who?
twerarte	everyone, all
nge+rteye?	what about you?
eylwekere,	
mentye anewene!	poor thing, leave him alone!

Palatal sounds

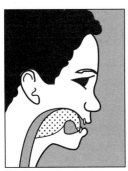 These sounds are a little bit like the English **ch** or **j** sounds. They are made by touching the tip of your tongue onto the bottom of your lower teeth and pushing the top part of your tongue tip against the front part of the roof of the mouth.

Sounds spelt with the letters ***ny***

This sound is a bit like the **n** in 'onion'.

eylpertenye

 67   eylperte**ny**e   wedge-tailed eagle
         tyarle**ny**e   arm
         nyanye   mother's mother

There are also words which have **ty** following **ny**. This is written **nty** and never **nyty**

 68   arrkwe**nty**e   three
         arre**nty**e   devil

Further information
Try this tongue twister:

Arrantye arrenty-arenge arrenye

waterbag   devil - 's   over there

The devil's waterbag is over there

Now listen to **ny** when it is followed by **w**

 69

| tya**ny**wenge | tobacco |
| ma**ny**werne | loaded with fruit |

There are also words which have another consonant with **nyw**

 70

| a**nty**wempe | very dangerous snake |
| a**nty**we | humpy |

Sounds spelt with the letters ty

 71

a**ty**e	I
a**ty**enge	me
tyarlenye	arm

Now listen to **ty** when it is followed by **w**

 72

| **ty**wekere | dislike |
| a**ty**wetnpe | perentie |

Sounds spelt with the letters tny

 73

| a**tny**eme | witchetty bush |
| a**tny**emayte | witchetty grub |

atnyemayte

Note
nyty is always written **nty**, similarly **lyty** is written **lty** and **tnyty** is written **tnty**.

Listen to this word which has **ty** after **tny**

 74

| e**tnty**e | hair |

~~~~~~

Hint

The sounds **pm**, **tnh**, **rtn**, **tn**, **ytn**, **tny**, and **kng** are made by blocking the air in the mouth and then letting it flow through the nose. The **tny** sound in Kaytetye sounds a bit like **t'n ya** in the sentence 'eat'n ya food' if you say it with a strong Australian accent.

~~~~~~

Now listen to **tny** when it is followed by **w**

 75   atnywenke   (to) enter

Sounds spelt with the letters **ly**

This sound is a bit like the **ll** in 'million'.

 76   akelye   little
              pelyakwe   duck
              lyerrmewe   cold weather

There are also words which have another consonant with **ly**

 77   akaltye   knowledgeable
              altyarrenhe   become happy

Now listen to **ly** when it is followed by **w**

 78   lywekenke   (to) light fire
              alywerlpe   *Eucalyptus normantonensis*

Sounds spelt with the letter **y**

 79   ngayele   hungry
              anteyane   sitting
              yakwethe   bag

Now listen to **y** when it is followed by **w**

 80   ywerrpe   across, crossways
              ywekenke   (to) let out
              aywerle   *Acacia murrayana*

aywerle

 Useful expressions 6

              nthekelarte?   whereabouts?
              nyapertawe!   right here!
              tyangkwerre   just there
              arrenyawe   far over there

Velar sounds

These sounds are made with the back of the tongue held up to the back part of the mouth, in nearly the same place as where the **k** and **g** sounds are made in English.

Sounds spelt with the letter k

 81
kengkarrenke	(to) sneak up on
etak-etake	carefully
ake	head

Now listen to **k** when it is followed by **w**

 82
kwarte	egg
arr**kw**entye	three
Kwementyaye	(avoidance name)

Sounds spelt with the letters ng

 83
ngayele	hungry
atye**ng**e	me
artnwe**ng**e	child

artnwenge

Hint

You might need some practice saying **ng** at the beginning of words, because in English it only occurs in the middle and end of words. Practise saying 'singer' a few times, and at the same time try to cut off the first two sounds, so eventually you get to **nger**.

When **ng** is followed by **k** the sound is like that in 'fi**ng**er', 'mo**nk**ey' or 'do**nk**ey'.

 84
a**ngk**etye	foot
nga**ngk**aye	doctor
ntey**ngk**e	ripe

Now listen to **ng** when it is followed by **w**

 85
ngwenge	tomorrow

There are also words which have **k** with **ngw**. The **k** is always written before the **w**

 86
re**ngkw**e	don't know
arre**ngkw**e	mother
nthek-a**ngkw**erre	whereabouts

Sounds spelt with the letters kng

 87
a**kng**errake	east
arr**kng**e	blood
kngapetye	changed, turned

There are also words which have another consonant after **kng**

 88   ekngkelthele   nail, claw

Now listen to **kng** when it is followed by **w**

 89

Kngwarraye	(skin name)
kngwere	different, another
a**kng**we	deaf, mad

Sounds spelt with the letter *h*

Different speakers pronounce this letter differently—sometimes it sounds like the long vowel in the English word 'car'.

 90

aherre	kangaroo
ahentye	throat
aherrke	sun

Sounds spelt with the letter *w*

 91

ware	fire
wepe	spider
awerre	boy, male

wepe

Listen to the difference between the following sets of words

 92

artnpenke	(to) run
atnpenke	(to) touch

Useful expressions 7

nthakenhaye?	what's up?
ahen-apeke?	is that OK? do you think so? are you OK?
yawe-yawe, ahene	yes, it's OK, I agree
rwengkawe!	search me!
kartarte nge angkene	talk slower

93

artenke	(to) chop
atenke	(to) press

94

arlperre	whitewood tree
alperre	foliage
aylperre	fish

95

eylkwe	armpit
erlkwe	old man

Vowels

You may have noticed that so far you have only seen two vowels written in Kaytetye: **a** and **e**. Although these are the only two letters we use to write the Kaytetye vowel sounds, both are heavily influenced by the consonant sounds in the word.

Sounds spelt with the letter *a*

(i) When **a** is heard in the middle of a word it is pronounced like the **a** in 'father'

 96

mataye	clouds
errpmalhe	smoke
ware	fire

(ii) Listen to how **a** sounds when it comes before **rt**, **rn**, **rtn** and **rl** in a word

97

apmarleye	my uncle
mwekarte	hat
arntwe	water

(iii) Listen to how **a** sounds when it comes at the start of a word

98

akelye	little
akwelye	rain
anatye	yam

Note

In Kaytetye there are many words that start with an **a**, but you do not always have to say the **a**. For example, you can say **akelye** or **kelye** and they both mean 'little'. However, there are also words where you must say the **a** because if you leave it off, the word has a different meaning. You saw some examples on page 11; other examples are: **atyerre** 'younger sibling' but **tyerre** 'maggots'; **kwerrke** 'small hole' but **akwerrke** 'baby, child'.

If you're trying to decide whether to write a word with an **a**, it helps to remember the following principles:

- If you *can* say **a** on the beginning of a word, even though you often don't, always write it with an **a**.
- If you *never* say **a** on the beginning of a word, don't write it with an **a**.

(iv) Listen to how **a** sounds when it comes before **yt**, **yn**, **ytn** and **yl**

 99

ayleme	we two
Kaytetye	Kaytetye
aynenke	(to) eat

aynenke

(v) Listen to how **a** sounds when it occurs before a **w**

 100   kartawarre   root
             arawerrenge   worried, anxious

Sounds spelt with the letter *e*

(i) When **e** is heard in the middle or at the start of a word it is pronounced like the **e** in 'hermit'

 101   nthekele   where
             nthelarte   that
             eletnhenke   (to) throw

(ii) Listen to how **e** sounds when it comes before **rt**, **rn** and **rl** in a word

 102   mperlarte   like that
             errtywerne   tooth

(iii) When **e** comes before the letter **y** it sounds more like the English **ea** in the word 'heat'

 103   eyterrtye   body, person
             eylkwennge   mouse
             eylperalkere   sugarbag

(iv) Listen to how **e** sounds when it is followed by **w**, or by another consonant(s) and then **w**

 104   errpwerle   black, dark
             errwele   top, high
             ethwe   poison

(v) Notice how the **e** following **w** can also sound different

 105   amwelye   bearded dragon
             mwekarte   hat
             arrengkwe   mother

amwelye

One thing you may have noticed about Kaytetye is that all the words end with **e**. This vowel is not always pronounced, but it is always written, so a word such as **aleme** can be pronounced either a-LEM, a-LEM-a, or a-LEM-e. Similarly, when speech flows smoothly in Kaytetye the final **e** on words is not heard if the next word starts with a vowel: for example the following sentence, which is written

 106   Artweye nharte apenhe(-rre) eyntemaperte
          man   that   went   for good
          That man went for good

actually sounds more like this:
          Artwey anhart apenh eyntemaperte

Stress and syllables

Words can be divided into smaller parts called *syllables*. Each vowel is the centre of a syllable. You can count the number of syllables if you tap your hand while you say the word slowly, for example 'ru.nning, al.li.ga.tor'. (Here dots are used to separate syllables.)

One syllable of a word is usually pronounced louder and in a higher voice than the others. This syllable is said to be stressed. A difference in stress makes a word sound strange. In some cases—such as the difference between the two words permit (I per.MIT you to do it) and permit (a liquor PER.mit)—a difference in stress can change the meaning. (In these examples the capital letters represent the stressed syllable.) In Kaytetye the stressed syllable in a word is usually the first syllable that starts with a consonant, for example

 107

alperre	leaf	al.PE.rre
arwele	stick, tree	a.RWE.le
kwarte	egg	KWA.rte

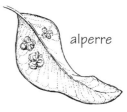

alperre

Hyphens

Many Kaytetye words are made up of lots of different parts or endings and so can be quite long. In order to make it easier to read Kaytetye, people decided to put hyphens between the parts of words to break them up. For example, it is easier to read

 108   Thangkenhareng-areny-amerne
The people belonging to Thangkenharenge

than

Thangkenharengarenyamerne

Some speakers of Kaytetye and other Arandic languages who are literate in their language write endings as separate words, or sometimes join them together without a hyphen. However, in this learner's guide, which is aimed at English speakers and readers, endings are joined with a hyphen to show how endings relate to the word which they follow.

In Kaytetye, all words are written with a final **e**. When an ending is joined to a word, either with or without a hyphen, then the final **e** of the word is dropped if the ending starts with a vowel (a or e). For example **artnwenge** plus **-aperte** becomes **artnweng-aperte** and **artnwenge** + **-arre** becomes **artnwengarre**.

Thus:

> Thangkenhareng**e**-areny**e**-amerne
>
> is written as
>
> Thangkenhareng-areny-amerne

This also makes it easier for English speakers learning to read Kaytetye, as **e** on the end of a word isn't pronounced before endings starting with a vowel.

The general rules about when and when not to use hyphens are as follows:

- hyphens are used to break up doubled up words such as **anaty-anatye** 'heart', **arlkeny-arlkenye** 'striped'.

- They are used before long endings (two syllables or more) if the start of the word is also long (two syllables or more). For example **aleke** 'dog' plus the ending -**ketye** 'because of' is written as **aleke-ketye** 'because of the dogs'.

- Kaytetye verbs can be made up of several verbs joined together. Hyphens are used to break up verbs that are made of several parts, or that have long endings on them, for example **angkerr-aperrane** 'talking while going along'.

- Hyphens are *not* used when the ending is short or the word itself is short. For example, the combination of the word **arntwe** 'water' and the ending -**penhe** 'from, after' is written as **arntwepenhe**, 'after the rain'. Similarly, the word **artnwenge** 'child' plus +**arre** becomes **artnwengarre** and **erlkwe** 'old man' plus the ending +**nge** is written as **erlkwenge**. Notice how the **we** of **erlkwe** changes to an **oo** sound if there is an ending after the **we**.

More useful expressions

Questions and commands

Here are some simple questions and commands to use as you begin talking with Kaytetye speakers. Learn them off by heart. You might not understand how the sentences are put together, but don't worry. You will learn this as you go through the course.

angken-apertame nge	say it again
apenerne ngawe	come here
atyengelke elpathewethe	now listen to me
elpathene nte	listen
etnyene nte	give it here
kartarte nge angkene	say it slower
me	here it is; here take this
mentye anewene	leave it
mpe	let's go
tyelarte nge anene	sit down here
arrenentye?	how many?
elewarte?	when?
kngwer-angkwerre nge angkene?	say it another way?
lwarre?	really? is that so?
nhantarte nhartepe?	who is that?
tnhante?	who?
nthakenhe?	how? what?
nthakenhe kaytetyelepe arntwewene...?	how do you say...in Kaytetye?
nthakenhe nge angkene...?	how do you say...?
ntheke?	where?
wantartaye?	what's up?
wantewe?	why? what for?
wante-rtame...?	what does...mean?

Further information
The verb **elpathenke** 'to hear' also means 'to understand'. You might hear people say that they can 'hear' Kaytetye but not speak it, meaning that they understand it, but don't speak it.

Learning hints
• In this section you have learnt many new sounds. Go back and practise saying the Kaytetye words in this section and then listen to the CD to see how well you can pronounce them.

• Memorise all the useful expressions and practise saying them throughout the course in response to the dialogues and example sentences you hear.

Part three: the lessons

Dialogue 1   Arlelke

Listen to the following conversation on the CD. You will hear it twice, the second
time you play the part of the second speaker, Ngale.

Vocabulary			
alele	soon, wait	ayenge	I
arlelke	hunting	nge	you (*singular*)
apenke	go	ntheke	where
apenkerne	come	nthek-angkwerre	whereabouts

Note

Sometimes the extra bit +**awe** or +**aye** is added to make the speech stronger or more emphatic—it's like the English exclamation 'hey!'. The ending +**awe** is commonly heard with **apeyakele** and **alkaperte**, as in **alkapertawe!** 'alright!', and **apeyakelawe!** 'No, nothing!'. The ending +**aye** is often heard on the end of kinship words. The word **yekaye!** 'wow!' is also made up from this ending. Both +**awe** and +**aye** are glossed 'hey'.

Remember for short endings like these, the **e** is deleted from the previous word. So **nge** 'you' plus +**awe** 'hey' becomes **ngawe!** 'hey you!'

1.1 Noun endings

There are many *endings* in Kaytetye that go on words to change their meaning in some way. Some endings go only on verbs, some go only on nouns while others can go on both. Kaytetye *nouns* are words for things and words that describe things; they are equivalent not only to English nouns—words for things, like 'shop' 'rock' 'person' or 'Alice Springs'—but also to English *adjectives*—words that describe things, such as 'black', 'thin' or 'happy'.

Endings that go on nouns can show such things as direction, location, possession, similarity and many other things. These endings are often used in situations where English uses *prepositions* (those small words such as 'to', 'from', 'through', 'in', 'on', 'at' and 'by').

In Kaytetye there are no prepositions. Instead, you have to learn which type of ending to put on the noun. For example:

 1　　Thangkenharenge-theye　　from Thangkenharenge

Further information

Thangkenharenge is the name of the Barrow Creek area. It is also the name of the Aboriginal corporation based at Barrow Creek which represents mostly Kaytetye people. The name is made up of these parts:

thangkerne 'bird' plus the ending -**arenge** 'belonging to'

and literally means '(the country) belonging to the bird'.

Notice that the place name is not spelt exactly as it sounds (Thangkerne) but

Thangkenhe, which is an old spelling that has been kept. It is often the case that the spelling of place names is different from the spelling of the words they come from. A more extreme example is the community which is sometimes spelt Ali-Curung (formerly Warrabri) although it should be spelt **Alekarenge**

Alek-arenge

dog-'s

which means '(the country) belonging to the dog'.

1.2 'through', 'around'

The first noun ending you will learn is **-angkwerre**. In dialogue 1 you heard it in **nthek-angkwerre nge apenke+aye** 'where(abouts) are you going'. It is used to say 'around, in the area of' as in 'it happened around the hills'. This ending is also used to say 'through', or 'via' a place, as in 'I went through Ti-Tree'. Listen to the following examples and try to get a feel for the meaning of **-angkwerre**.

2   Nthek-**angkwerre** nge apenkaye?

where-through   you go+hey

Where are you going?

3   *Bush*-**angkwerre** re   apenke

bush-through   he   goes

He is going through the bush

4   Re atnhelengkwe atnenty-**angkwerre** rntwenke

he emu   throat-through   cuts

He cuts the emu across the neck

5   Antarrengenye-warle atanthe apenke Elerewarr-**angkwerre**

Antarrengenye-to   they   go   Elerewarre-through

They are going to Antarrengenye via Elerewarre

Note

Remember the final vowel of a word isn't heard when the next word starts with a vowel, so a phrase such as **nge apenke** 'you go' sounds more like **ng‿apenke**.

1.3 Verbs and verb endings

Verbs are words like 'hit', 'eat' and 'run'. They show what sort of action, state and process is taking place. Mastering the use of Kaytetye verbs is one of the most important things to do when learning the language, because the Kaytetye verb carries much of the important meaning in a sentence: you can't say much without them.

The verbs can also become very complicated, with many extra bits or endings added to the *stem* of the verb to elaborate on its meaning. Endings that go on verbs say things about the action—such as when it happened, whether the action is ongoing and the direction of the action. Usually the endings go straight on the verb stem, but sometimes the actual verb stem itself changes. Verb stems are not heard on their own; they must have an ending on them. Some Kaytetye verb stems are listed below. They are written with a plus to show that an ending must follow.

ane+   sit
ape+   go
ayne+   eat

1.4   Doing something now [present tense]

In the above dialogue you heard the ending +**nke** on the verb **ape**+ 'go'. This shows that the event or action happens now, or it happens habitually. It is called the present tense ending. Like the English present tense, in Kaytetye it can also be used if something is about to happen soon. Listen to the following example sentences which all have verbs in the present tense.

6   Nthek-angkwerre nge apenke?
     where-through   you go
     Where are you going?

7   Alele ayenge apenke+rne
     wait   I   go+this way
     Wait, I'm coming

8   Artnte+nge re anenke
     rock+on   he sits
     He sits on the rock

9   Artweye apenke ngwetyanpe
     man   go   morning
     The man goes in the morning

Note
+**nke** is pronounced +**rnke** when the preceding consonant is any of the consonants in columns 3, 4 and 5 of Table 1 on page 10.

1.5 'come' and 'go'

You heard in dialogue 1 both **apenke** 'go' and **apenkerne** 'come'. Note how the stem, **ape-**, is the same in both these words. The only difference between them is that 'come' has another ending, +**rne**, after the present tense ending. It literally means 'this way', or 'movement towards the speaker'. It can also occur on certain other motion verbs to show that the movement is towards the speaker. This ending is always the last ending on the verb. If the verb is in the past tense then +**rne** becomes -**ngerne**.

10   Arwele+le   alarre+nhe-**ngerne**   re   mwetekaye
         stick+with   hit+PAST-this way   he/she   car
         He/she hit the car with a stick

11   Athe nharte mwernarte ampe+nhe-**ngerne**
         grass   that   this side   burnt+PAST-this way
         The grass burnt this way

Note

The word **alarrenke** in Kaytetye can mean either 'hit' or 'kill' depending on the context.

1.6 Focus marker

One of the most frequently heard endings in Kaytetye is +**pe**, which is used to emphasise a word. For example, in dialogue 1 you heard **nge** followed by +**pe**, where it signified 'Are *you* coming?'. Listen for where it occurs on the CD in 'Test your skill 1'. It occurs on both nouns and verbs and you will hear it a lot throughout this course.

Test your skill 1

Listen to dialogue 1 again. Write down the Kaytetye, and an English translation for it.

 Listen to these Kaytetye sentences on the CD and repeat them to yourself. Work out their meaning in English.

1   Nthek-angkwerre re apenke?

2   Nthek-angkwerre nge apenke?

3   Nthek-angkwerre artweye apenke?

4   Ngepe apenkerne?

5   Repe apenkerne?

6   Artweye apenkerne?

7   Ayenge apenke *bush*-angkwerre.

8   Re apenke Alekareng-angkwerre.

9   Ngepe apenke *Alice-Springs*-angkwerre?

10   Artweye apenke Thangkenhareng-angkwerre.

11   Aleke artnpenke apmer-angkwerre.

12   *Bush*-angkwerre atnhelengkwe+we arlelke aynanthe apenke.

13   Ayenge apenkerne ngwetyanpe.

Learning hint
At this stage go back and revise, and don't go on until you have learnt this part of the lesson off by heart, so that when the next new feature is added below, you are building on a firm foundation.

Dialogue 2   Wante nyartepe?

Vocabulary

aherre	kangaroo	atnwenthe	meat
anatye	yam	ngkwarle	sweet food
nharte	that	rlwene	tucker
nyarte	this	thangkerne	bird
arwele	tree, stick	wante	what
atetherre	budgerigar	yerrkeyerre	edible lerp from blue
atnkerre	coolibah tree		mallee tree

2.1   'this' and 'that', 'here' and 'there'

In Kaytetye the word for 'this' also means 'here', and the word for 'that' also means 'there'. These words are called *demonstratives*.

nyarte   this, here
nharte   that, there

Note
Sometimes an **a** can be heard on the beginning of these words, so they sound more like **anyarte** and **anharte**; however, they are always written without the initial **a**.

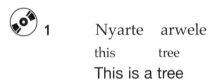

1   Nyarte   arwele
     this   tree
     This is a tree

2   Nharte   artnwenge
     that   child
     That is a child

Note
The order of the words in the above example sentences could be changed around without the meaning being affected much. So **artnwenge nyarte** can mean 'this is a child' or 'this child'.

Demonstratives can get quite complex. You will learn more about them in chapter 6.

Note

Look at the last part of dialogue 2. It is also possible to say **wante nhamernarte** 'what are *they*' instead of **wante nhartepe** 'what is *that*' if you are talking about more than one thing. Plural 'this' and 'that' will be discussed further in chapter 6.

2.2 'is', 'be' and verbless sentences

From dialogue 2 you can see that it is not always necessary to have a verb in order to form a sentence in Kaytetye. You might also have noticed that in the dialogue there is no verb in Kaytetye corresponding to the English verb 'to be' and its other forms such as 'is', 'are', 'were', 'was' and 'will be'. In Kaytetye if you want to say 'this is a dog' you can just say 'this dog'.

3   Nyarte   artnwenge   akelye

this   child   small

This is a small child/This child is small

4   Nharte   artnte   alkenhe

that   hill   big

That is a big hill/That hill is big

5   Ayenge   kwetnaye

I   tired

I'm tired

Alhwenge akelye

6   Alhwenge akelye   kwereyenge

hole   small   his

His hole is small

Verbless sentences refer to states of affairs in the present time only—that is, the time when something is said. To refer to past or future time a verb must be used. So:

Ayenge   kwetnaye

I   tired

I am tired

Ayenge   kwetnaye   **anenhe**

I   tired   sat

I was tired

Other ways of saying 'is', 'are', 'were' etc. will be covered in chapter 6.

2.3 Categorising words [classifiers]

In Kaytetye, unlike English, it is common to put a categorising noun, a *classifier*, before the thing you are talking about, so instead of saying **aherre** 'kangaroo' you say **atnwenthe aherre** 'meat kangaroo'. Kaytetye has no single word that corresponds to 'food' in English; instead you must specify what sort of food it is. The following classifiers refer to different classes of food, or the function of things (for example by using or not using **kayte** you can distinguish between edible and non-edible grubs). These classifiers are used commonly in Kaytetye. Identify the ones used in dialogue 2.

7	enye/rlwene	vegetable, fruit and bread foods
8	atnwenthe/weye	meat, dairy products
9	kayte	edible grubs
10	ngkwarle	sweet foods (e.g. honey, nectar, sugarbag)
11	nterrenge	edible seeds

Note
You might have noticed that **thangkerne** and **arwele** were also used as categorising words in dialogue 2. Watch out for other nouns which are used as classifiers as you go through the course.

Sometimes it is only by using classifiers that you can distinguish between the plant and its food, for example:

12	arwele anatye	yam plant (*Ipomoea costata*)
13	rlwene anatye	yam, bush potato

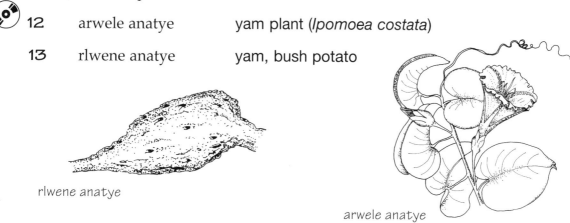

rlwene anatye

arwele anatye

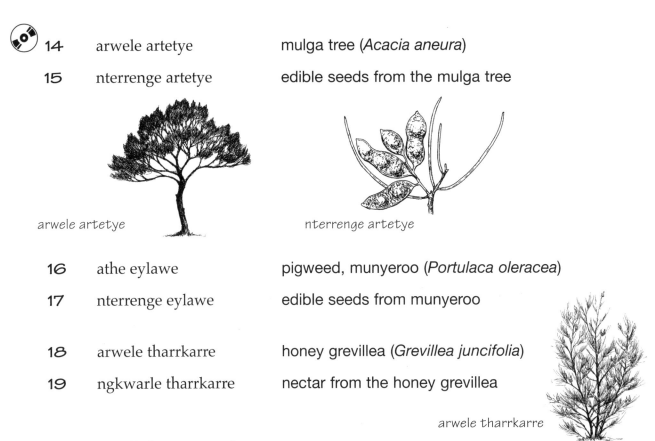

14   arwele artetye   mulga tree (*Acacia aneura*)

15   nterrenge artetye   edible seeds from the mulga tree

arwele artetye   *nterrenge artetye*

16   athe eylawe   pigweed, munyeroo (*Portulaca oleracea*)

17   nterrenge eylawe   edible seeds from munyeroo

18   arwele tharrkarre   honey grevillea (*Grevillea juncifolia*)

19   ngkwarle tharrkarre   nectar from the honey grevillea

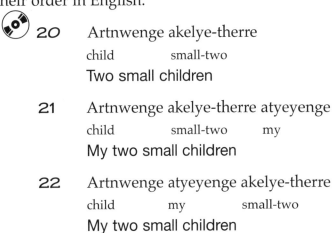

arwele tharrkarre

2.4   Describing words

In Kaytetye *describing words* such as **alkenhe** 'big', or **therre** 'two' follow the thing that they are describing. From the dialogue, you can see that the two words **anatye** and **alkenhe** are always next to each other and that **alkenhe** always follows **anatye**, even while the other words in the sentence change order quite freely. It would be incorrect to say **alkenhe anatye**. So unlike English, in Kaytetye the thing described always comes *before* the describing word.

Listen to these examples, where the order of the describing words is the opposite of their order in English.

20   Artnwenge akelye-therre
    child   small-two
    Two small children

21   Artnwenge akelye-therre atyeyenge
    child   small-two   my
    My two small children

22   Artnwenge atyeyenge akelye-therre
    child   my   small-two
    My two small children

In the examples above you can see that the word order in Kaytetye is the reverse of the word order in a similar English phrase.

2.5   How to say that there are more than one of something [plural]

On their own, Kaytetye words can be both *singular* and *plural*. A word such as **artnwenge** 'child' can mean both 'child' and 'children'. However, sometimes it is necessary to specify exactly what is meant. In English we usually put **s** on the end of the word to show that there is more than one of them, but in Kaytetye there are three different ways to say this. In Kaytetye you must specify if there are two, more than two, or a group of things where the things are viewed as a whole.

-therre	two
-amerne	many, some
-eynenge	lots, all of

You heard two of these endings in dialogue 2: **ngeymarr-*eynenge*** and **atnkerr-*amerne***. These endings go on the end of nouns.

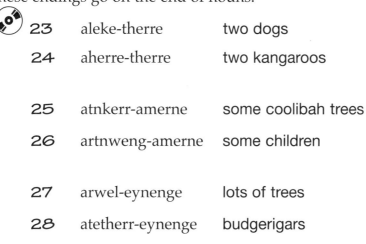

	23	aleke-therre	two dogs
	24	aherre-therre	two kangaroos
	25	atnkerr-amerne	some coolibah trees
	26	artnweng-amerne	some children
	27	arwel-eynenge	lots of trees
	28	atetherr-eynenge	budgerigars

There are only a few numbers in Kaytetye:

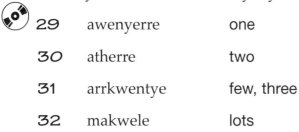

	29	awenyerre	one
	30	atherre	two
	31	arrkwentye	few, three
	32	makwele	lots

Notice how **therre** is both an ending and a word which can stand on its own, meaning 'two'. In this case it is spelt **atherre**.

Beware
Don't confuse **arrkwentye** 'few' with **errkwentye** 'policeman'.

Test your skill 2

Listen to dialogue 2 again. Write down the Kaytetye, and an English translation for it.

 Listen to these Kaytetye sentences on the CD and repeat them. Work out their meaning in English.

1   Wante nhartepe?
2   Nyartepe elpaye akelye.
3   Wante nyartepe?
4   Nhartepe aleke alkenhe.
5   Wante nhartepe?
6   Nyartepe arwele akelye.
7   Wante nyartepe?
8   Nhartepe artnte alkenhe.
9   Aleke errpwerle alkenhe-therre.
10   Artnwenge akely-eynenge.
11   Arelhe-therre apenke apmere-warle.
12   Artwey-amerne apenke arlelke aherrewe.

The following words are types of foods. Put the right food word from section 2.3 in front of these words (**rlwene/enye, atnwenthe/weye, kayte, ngkwarle** or **nterrenge**). You may need to check the alphabetical listing in the back of this book.

atnwenthe   pweleke

_____   anatye

_____   areynenge

_____   aparle

_____   wampere

_____   arlkerre

_____ alkwarreye

_____ eylpweralke

_____ atnyemayte

_____ aherre

Learning hint

Make sure you are using the useful phrases on page 31 as you go through the course. Go back and revise them now if you can't remember them.

Dialogue 3 Mwanyeme

Vocabulary

anteyane	sitting, staying	ngkwarle-maynteye,	
enye	tucker	mwanyeme	type of bush
aynanthe	we (more than two)		fruit that grows
elpaye	creek		in creeks
errwanthe	you mob		(*Solanum*
ngwenge	tomorrow		*cleistogamum*)

Further information

Ngkwarle-maynteye (*Solanum cleistogamum*) is a fruit that grows on small bushes around creek and river banks. These days only older people use this word: **mwanyeme** is the word more commonly heard today.

Elpaye is the Kaytetye word for river or creek. In Central Australia these are dry, sandy watercourses—usually they do not have water in them.

3.1 'to', 'towards'

To say that you are going *to* a place, person or thing, you use the ending **-warle**. You heard this ending added to **elpaye** 'creek' in dialogue 3. It can be translated as 'to' or 'towards'.

 1   Aleke artnpenke apmere-**warle**

dog   runs   camp-to

The dog runs towards the camp

2   Ayenge apmere-**warle** alpe+wethe

        I   camp-to   go back+PURP

    I'm going back to the camp

3   Nthek**arle**?

    Where to?

Note

Often the ending **-warle** is shortened to +**arle**. In this case it is not hyphenated onto the noun. (Nouns are explained in section 1.1.)

In dialogue 1 we saw that **nthek-angkwerre apenke?** means 'where are you going?' Another way of saying this is with the ending **-warle** instead of **-angkwerre**. This is frequently followed by the ending **-arte** (discussed in 6.2), so: **ntheke***warl***arte apenke?** 'Where are you going?'

'into', 'onto'

The ending -**warle** has many other meanings too. It is used to show the goal or end point of an action that involves motion. Here it translates as 'into', 'onto' or 'to'.

4   Arrengkwe+le artnwenge-**warle** arntwe yathenke

    mother+DOER   child-to   water   pours

    The mother pours water onto the child

5   Atyelarte weyepe   alpenhe   eylpere-**warle**

    here+DEM   meat+FOCUS went back   hollow tree-to

    Here an animal went back into a hollow tree

6   Artweye apenherre elpaye-**warle** angketye ampelare+wethe

    man   went   creek-to   foot   see tracks+PURP

    A man goes to look for tracks at the creek

7   Weye (re) eletnhenke apmere kwereyeng**arle**

    meat he puts down   camp   his+in

    He puts the meat down in his camp

Note

Sometimes, the second time you hear the example sentence the word order is slightly different from the first. This does not change the meaning of the phrase.

In example 7, you heard one speaker leave out the word **re** on the CD. Both ways of saying the sentence are correct, and there are more examples of optional words throughout the learner's guide. They are enclosed in brackets, like **(re)** on page 48.

'out of'

The ending -**warle** is also used to describe removal or seperation of an object. Here it translates as 'out of', 'off'.

8   Etntye**warle** atyewenhe nyarte alheyle+wethe

   hair+to   myself   this   pull+PURP

   I'll pull this out of my hair

9   Pwete atyewenhe-**warle** angketye-**warle** alheyle+wethe

   shoe   myself-to   foot-to   pull+PURP

   I'll pull the shoe off my foot

Note

Endings like -**warle** can go on more than one word when more than one word is used to describe something. In example 9, -**warle** goes on both 'my' and 'foot'.

3.2   'for' [dative ending]

The ending +**we** has many uses in Kaytetye. One of the simplest of these uses is to show the purpose of an action, or who the action is being done to, or what an action is being done for—just as it was used in dialogue 3 to mean 'going hunting *for* bush fruit'. It may be translated as 'for', 'at', 'with' 'to' or 'into'. This ending is attached to nouns.

10   wante**we**?

   what+for

   What for?

11   Aynanthe kayte**we** apenke

   we   grub+for   go

   We are going for (witchetty) grubs

12   Arelhe+le   artnwenge akelye**we**   enye pwenke

   woman+DOER   child   small+for   food   cook

   The woman is cooking food for the child

The ending **+we** can go on the end of a thing or person that a feeling or thought is directed towards.

13 Kwerre nharte ahengarrerane kwerre atyeyenge**we**
girl that getting angry girl mine+for
That girl is getting angry with my girl

14 Ngkwarle**we** ayenge tywekere
sweet+for I dislike
I don't like sweet things/grog

Beware
Kaytetye object pronouns (see page 70), such as **atyenge** 'me', also mean 'for me' so they cannot take the **-we** ending.

---

15 Ayenge apmere**we** altherarrenke
I country+for get homesick
I'm homesick for (my) country

16 Kwere-penhe apenhe-ngerne kwenyele-penhe**we**
it-after went-this way yesterday-after+for
Since then he has come here about yesterday's business

To say where the object or receiver of an action is, either **-warle** or **+we** can be used. It is best translated as 'on', 'at', 'in', 'by' or even 'from' or 'off'. In the following sentences either **-warle** or **+we** can be used.

17 Ahakeye (re) elye**warle** kwenke
bush plum he shade+in swallows
He eats bush plums <u>in the shade</u>

18 Twepe-twepe re rntwenke arwele alkenhe**we**
around s/he picks tree big+for
She picks them <u>off a big bush</u>

19 Artnwenge ngkeyenge atye arenhe apmere-**warle**
child your I saw camp-to
I saw your child <u>at the camp</u>

20 Ampelarenhe angketye apmere kngwere-**warle**
saw tracks footprints place another-to
They saw tracks <u>at another place</u>

21 Re kwere apmere**warle** ayney-alpenke
he it camp-for eats-goes back and
He goes back and eats it <u>in camp</u>

Note
In section 6.1 you will learn more ways of showing location.

3.3 More about noun endings

In Kaytetye there are many noun endings (like **-angkwerre**) whose meanings are similar to prepositions in English—words like 'in', 'at', 'from', 'to', 'through'. In chapter 2 you learnt how nouns can be used as adjectives and classifiers, such as **aleke errpwerle alkenhe** 'the big black dog'.

If there is a group of words describing a single thing or person, then the endings talked about in this section go on the last word in the group.

 22   apmere kwereyenge-**warle**

　　　camp   his+to

　　　to his camp

23   artnwenge akelye-**therrewe**

　　　child   small-two+for

　　　for the two small children

24   artnte   errpwerl-amern-**angkwerre**

　　　rock/hill black-many-through

　　　through the black rocks

apmere kwereyenge-warle

In this case the endings go on the end of the phrase. It would be incorrect to say:

✗   apmere-**warle** kwereyenge

　　camp+to his

✗   artnwenge**we** akelye-therre

　　child+for   small-two

✗   artnte-**angkwerre** errpwerl-amerne

　　rocks-through   black-many

Although it is not incorrect to put the ending after every word in the phrase, it really isn't necessary and mostly people tend not to do it, they just put it after the last word.

3.4 'will' [future tense]

The most common way of saying that something will happen is by putting the ending +**ye** or +**yerre** on the verb stem.

 25   Ngwenge ayenge ape+**yerre**

　　　tomorrow   I   go-will

　　　I will go tomorrow

26   Atye kwere are**yerre**

I   him   see+will

I will see him

27   Arntetyarre**ye**+lke ayenge

sick+will+now   I

Now I will get sick

Note

Some people put +**rre** on the end of the future tense of the verb, so **enweye** becomes **enweyerre**, **aneye** becomes **aneyerre**, etc. This does not change the meaning of the word.

In chapter 1 we saw that the straight present tense ending +**nke** is used if something is just about to happen, whereas +**ye** is used if something will happen in the more distant future.

 28   Alele ayenge ape**nke**

soon   I   go

I'm going soon

29   Ngwenge ayenge ape**nke**

soon   I   go

I will go tomorrow

Note

The future tense ending of **apenkerne** 'come' is not **apeyerne** but **aperrenenyeye** 'will come'. Luckily this is one of the very few Kaytetye irregular verbs.

3.5   Putting a group of words together [word order]

We saw in chapter 2 how a group of nouns have to be in a certain order—that is, with the descriptive words following the thing that is being described. Now we will look at how to construct a sentence which has nouns and verbs. To a learner of Kaytetye it can seem that there is no set order at all in a Kaytetye sentence, or that the order is often completely different from that in an English sentence. For example:

 30   Artnwenge+le aleke akelye alarre+nhe

child+DOER   dog   small   hit+PAST

The child hit the little dog

Without changing the meaning of the sentence, and still remaining grammatically correct in Kaytetye, you can change the order of the words in the above sentence in the following ways:

 31   **Aleke akelye** artnwengele alarrenhe

       Aleke akelye alarrenhe artnwengele

       Alarrenhe **aleke akelye** artnwengele

       Alarrenhe artnwengele **aleke akelye**

       Artnwengele alarrenhe **aleke akelye**

In English, word order is very important in showing meaning: for example 'the child hit the dog' means something entirely different from 'the dog hit the child', even though there are exactly the same words in the sentence. In general, the order of Kaytetye words in a sentence is quite free. It is the endings on the words, rather than the word order, which tell you who did what to whom. But although all the above variations are grammatically correct, the most usual order is for the verb to come last or late in a Kaytetye sentence.

Learning hint
To speak Kaytetye well, you must learn to free yourself from English word order. A good way to do this is to practise saying the one Kaytetye sentence with all the various possible word orders. Try this in the exercises at the end of each lesson.

Further information
There is a tendency in Kaytetye for the pronouns to be the second word in a sentence, as in the examples below.

    Arltepe   re   pwenke-rtame

    big guts+FOCUS   he   cooks-EMPH

    He cooks the big guts

    Tyangkwerre re   tnenty-tnentye apenhe-ngerne

    this way   he   noisy   came-this way

    I heard him coming this way

Test your skill 3

Listen to dialogue 3 again. Write down the Kaytetye, and an English translation for it.

 Listen to these Kaytetye sentences on the CD and repeat them to yourself. Work out their meaning in English.

1   Ayenge elpaye-warle apenke.

2   Artweye apenke apmere-warle.

3   Atnwenthe nyarte aleke+we.

4   Aynanthe apenke arlkerre+we.

5   Ayenge apeye elpaye alkenhe-warle.

6   Arelhe alpeye apmere-warle.

7   Aynanthe apenke elpaye-warle ngkwarle-maynteye+we.

8   Atye arntwe yathenke pakete-warle.

9   Atye arntarrtyenke elpaye-warle kalyeyampe.

10   Atye arenhe(rre) antywe+warle ngeymarre.

11   Atye aleke arenke elye+warle.

12   Ayenge eyntemarte aneyerre.

13   Kwenyele artwerrpe aynanthe apenhe elpay+arle.

Write the following Kaytetye verbs in both the past and future tense, then say them out loud:

Present tense

apenke	goes
_____	comes
_____	eats
_____	cooks
_____	pours
_____	cuts
_____	puts

Future tense

apeye / apeyerre	will go
_____	will come
_____	will eat
_____	will cook
_____	will pour
_____	will cut
_____	will put

Dialogue 4   Nthekarenye ngaye?

Vocabulary

alkaperte	OK, all right, finished	etnyenke	give
arntwe	water	kwathenhe	drank
atnkeleye	(male) cousin	me!	here!
atye	I	ngkawele	your uncle
nte	you (*singular, doer*)	nthakenharrerane	what's up?
atyenge	me	ntyerrel-arrerane	thirsty
atyeyenge	my	yewe-yewe	yes
aweleye	(my) uncle		

Further information

Artarre is a community near Neutral Junction Station. **Artarre** means 'emu tail feathers'. The country where Neutral Junction Station is, which is on the other side of the creek, is **Artwey-elperlaytnenge**.

It means 'where the men whistled' and also refers to the nearby spring.

4.1 'after', 'from'

To say that something happened after something else, or because of, or from something else, you use the noun ending **-penhe**, so **wante-penhe** 'what's up?' is literally 'from what'. It can also be used to indicate the cause of a certain event and can go on place names to show where something comes from, as well as the origin or source of something. Listen to and repeat the following examples which have **-penhe** in them, then try making up your own sentences with **-penhe**.

1 Kwere-**penhe** arntwelke re eylenke

   it-after   water+now s/he gets

   After that he gets some water

2 Arntwe-**penhe**+le re alhwenge angenke

   water-after+DOER   s/he hole   digs

   After having a drink he digs a hole

3 Elkeparre-**penhe** re apenke

   hibernate-after   s/he goes

   After hibernating he comes out

4 Ngkwarle-**penhe** re ampwarrenhe

   alcohol-after   s/he died

   He died from grog

5 Artetye-**penhe** kayle   mpwarenke

   mulga-after   boomerang made

   Boomerangs are made from mulga wood

Useful phrase
-penhe is often put on the end of the word **kwere** to make the word **kwere-penhe** which means 'then', 'after that' or 'and then'.

6 Kwere-**penhe** arwele perlape   twepe-twepe rntwenke

   it-after   tree   conkerberries around   picks

   Then she picks conkerberries all around the tree

4.2 'comes from', 'belongs to'

In dialogue 4 you heard the ending **-arenye** on place names and on the word for 'where'. This is the ending used to say that a person, animal or thing comes from, or belongs to, a particular place or country. When attached to a place name and used to describe a person, this usually indicates the person's origins, or that they have traditional connections to that place, or that they are closely associated with that place.

It can also refer to something or someone who is usually found in a place or closely associated with an organisation.

7   arnkenty-**arenye**

    single men's camp-ORIGIN

    single man

8   Areynenge artnt+**arenye**

    Euro   hills+ORIGIN

    Euros live in the hills

9   Arelhe nharte IAD-**arenye**

    woman that   IAD-ORIGIN

    That woman is from IAD

10   Arelhe Twerrp-**arenye** apenhe-ngerne

    woman Twerrpe-ORIGIN   went-this way

    The woman came from Twerrpe

11   Ayenge apmere ayerrer-**arenye**

    I   place   north-ORIGIN

    I'm from the north country

Useful phrase

ngarrp-arenye 'by oneself, alone'

    Atye entarenhe   atnhelengkwe ngarrp-arenye kwarte-warle

    I   saw someone go emu   alone-ORIGIN   egg-to

    I saw the emu go back by himself to the eggs

4.3   'now', 'then', 'next'

The ending +**lke** means 'now', 'then' or 'next' and can go on both nouns and verbs. If a sentence is in the past tense it means 'then' or 'just', in the present tense it means 'now' and in the future it means 'then' or 'next'. If it is on a noun it is best translated as 'now'. +**lke** can also go in the middle of words. When +**lke** combines with -**rtame** then it means 'in turn', 'next one'. -**rtame** on its own has a range of meanings, including adding emphasis.

12   Atwerrpe**lk**-arrenhe

    afternoon+then-became

    Then it got late

13   Rlengke**lke** ayenge angkenhe

    today+now   I   talked

    I just talked

14   Atye**lke** kwathe+wethe

    I+now   drink+PURP

    I want to drink water now

15   Rlengke**lke** angke+wethe

    today+now   talk+PURP

    Now we'll talk today

16   Elyewarle**lke** kwere alpereyneye(rre)

    shade+to+now   it   take back+will

    Then he will take it back into the shade

4.4   Transitive and intransitive verbs

In general, there are two types of Kaytetye verbs: *transitive* and *intransitive*. Intransitive verbs are generally ones where there is no recipient of the action, or the action of the verb does not directly affect something or someone. Typically verbs describing motion, spontaneous change, and human emotions are intransitive: 'sitting', 'going', 'swelling', 'being homesick', 'feeling happy' etc. Transitive verbs are those where an action is being done by someone to someone or something, or the action directly affects something else—such as 'eating', 'hitting', 'cooking'.

Note

You must be careful not to make assumptions about what is transitive and intransitive in Kaytetye from your understanding of English. For example the verb **aylenke** 'sing' is transitive in Kaytetye, and **ahentyarrenke** 'want' is intransitive in Kaytetye. In Kaytetye you must sing *something* so it is transitive. Wanting, however, is a state, as you do not have to want *something* in Kaytetye, so it is intransitive.

In English many verbs have both a transitive and an intransitive use, but in Kaytetye verbs are usually one or the other: there are only a few verbs in Kaytetye that can be both.

Some intransitive verbs include:

   17

ayenge apenke	I go
ayenge anenke	I sit, live, be
ayenge athamarrenke	I feel sorry for, miss

Some transitive verbs:

   18

atye etnyenke	I give
atye eylenke	I get
atye aynenke	I eat
atye pwenke	I cook
atye kwathenke	I drink

There are two important differences between sentences with a transitive verb and those with an intransitive verb, which will be covered in the next two sections.

4.5   The 'doer' marker

+le and *+nge* endings

The first thing that happens in a sentence with a transitive verb is that the 'doer' in the sentence, that is, the one that is performing the verb action (also called *actor*), is marked by the ending **+le**. But for short words—words with only one consonant or consonant cluster—the ending +**nge** is used instead of +**le**.

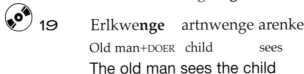

19   Erlkwe**nge**   artnwenge arenke

Old man+DOER   child   sees

The old man sees the child

20   Arelhe**le**   artnwenge arenke

woman+DOER child   sees

The woman sees the child

In English the order of the words in the sentence shows who is doing the action, but in Kaytetye the order of words is relatively free. Instead the endings +**nge**/+**le** show *who is doing what to whom*. Take the following examples:

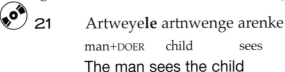

21   Artweye**le** artnwenge arenke

man+DOER   child   sees

The man sees the child

22   Artnwenge artweye**le** arenke

child   man+DOER sees

The man sees the child

Both of these sentences mean the same thing, and it is the +**le** on the end of **artweye** that shows us that the *man* is seeing, not the child.

If, however, **artnwenge** rather than **artweye** is marked with +**le**, the meaning changes:

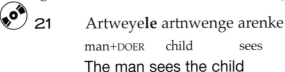

23   Artweye artnwenge**le** arenke

man   child+DOER   sees

The child sees the man

In this case the +**le** on the end of **artnwenge** shows us that the child is doing the looking. *It's essential to have +le on the right word or else you won't know who is doing what to whom.* Listen to and practise the following two sentences until you feel familiar with the +**le** ending.

24   Artnwenge aleke**le**   atnhenherre

child   dog+DOER bit

The dog bit the child

25   Artnwenge**le** aleke atnhenherre

child+DOER   dog   bit

The child bit the dog

Note

The endings +**le** and +**nge** have other functions too. Some of these are discussed further on in section 6.1.

'I' and 'you' as doers

The second thing is that the pronouns 'I' and 'you' change if they are doers: **ayenge** 'I' becomes **atye**, while **nge** 'you' becomes **nte**. You heard Thangale say **nte** in dialogue 4 when he said **kwathene nte** and you heard **atye** in the response **alkaperte atye kwathenhe**. This is because **kwathenke** '(to) drink' is a transitive verb.

Compare the following sentences where the pronouns change if the verb is transitive:

 26   **Ayenge** anenke

I   sitting

I sit

27   Atnwenthe **atye** aynenke

meat   I   eat

I eat meat

anenke

28   **Nge** anenke

you   sit

You sit

29   Atnwenthe **nte** aynenke

meat   you eat

You eat meat

Note

The +**nge**/+**le** does not go on pronouns if they are doers of the sentence. It would be incorrect to say:

✗   Atnwenthe <u>atanthe+nge</u> aynenke

They eat meat

✗   Atnwenthe <u>re+nge</u> aynenke

He eats meat

Fortunately for the learner of Kaytetye 'I' and 'you' are the only two pronouns that change depending on whether the verb is transitive or intransitive. All the other pronouns stay the same, for example:

30   **Re**   anenke

he/she sits

He/she sits

31   Atnwenthe **re**   aynenke

meat   he/she eats

He/she eats meat

32   **Errwanthe** anenke

you mob   sit

You lot sit

33   Atnwenthe **errwanthe** aynenke

meat   you mob   eat

You lot eat meat

4.6   Telling someone to do something [commands]

In English writing we use an exclamation mark to show that the words are being spoken in a forceful way, or that someone is making a *command*, or telling someone to do something. In English it can often sound quite rude to say things to people in this way, whereas in Kaytetye the command form of the verb, also called the *imperative*, is used frequently and is not impolite (though it does of course depend on who you are talking to and what you are telling them to do). In dialogue 4 you heard the command form of the verb 'to give', **etnyene**, and the command form of the verb 'to drink', **kwathene**.

To make a command in Kaytetye the ending +**ne** (which is glossed COMMAND) is added to the verb stem. Often the pronoun 'you' follows, so a command literally translates as 'Listen you!', 'Watch you!' or 'Drink you!' (**kwathene nte**), as you heard in dialogue 4. Remember, if the verb is transitive you will need to use the pronoun **nte** instead of **nge**.

Useful phrase

Angke**n**-apertame nge?

say+COMMAND-again   you

Can you say that again?

In Kaytetye there are many ways of saying 'you'. For example, there might be a group of people (you mob), two people (you two) or the 'you' might be a 'doer'. Pronouns are much more complicated in Kaytetye than in English, and they are dealt with later on in chapter 5.

Listen to and practise the following Kaytetye commands.

34 Elpathe**ne** nte!

listen+COMMAND you(DOER)

Listen!

35 Ayne**ne** nte!

eat+COMMAND you(DOER)

Eat!

36 Arntwe kwathe**ne** nte!

water drink+COMMAND you(DOER)

Drink the water!

37 Erlware**ne** errwanthe!

look+COMMAND you mob

Look (you mob)!

38 Anamarre**ne** ngaye!

move+COMMAND you+EMPH

Move!

39 Me, *medicine* nte kwathe**ne**!

here medicine you(DOER) drink+COMMAND

Here, drink the medicine

Note

For intransitive commands and questions some younger people use either **nte** or **nge** 'you', so for 'come here!' you can say either **apenerne nge!** or **apenerne nte!** Listen to whether '**nte**' or '**nge**' is sung in the Kaytetye song on CD2.

4.7 'must', 'have to'

Another way to tell someone that they should do something is to use the verb ending +**wene**. It shows that the verb action 'must', 'ought to', 'should' or 'is supposed to' happen. Sometimes +**wene** can simply be translated as 'let's do something'. It is also used as a more polite way to ask for something rather than using the imperative command +**ne**.

40 Errwanthe pweleke alwe**wene**!

you mob cattle chase+MUST

You're supposed to be chasing cattle!

41 Alpe**wene**+lke aynanthe apmere-warle

go back+MUST+now we place-to

Let's go back to camp now

~~~~~~

Useful phrase
    mentye anewene!   leave it alone!

~~~~~~

Test your skill 4

Listen to dialogue 4 again. Write down the Kaytetye, and an English translation for it.

 Listen to these Kaytetye sentences on the CD and repeat them to yourself. Work out their meaning in English.

1   Artnwenge+le artweye alarrenke.

2   Aherre artweye+le arenke.

3   Arrengkwe+le artnwenge+we etnyenke weye.

4   Weye aleke+le aynenke.

5   *Cool drink* kwathene nte!

6   Apene nge *town*-warle!

7   Artnte atyenge etnye+wene!

8   Warrke-penhe atanthe alpeye.

9   Kwere-penhe arntwe atye eylenke.

10   Atnkwe+penhe ayenge atntheyaytenke.

11   Aynanthe apeye *supper*-penhe.

12   Mwanyeme elpay-arenye.

13   Aweleye ayerrer-arenye.

14   Ayenge apmere atnteyerr-arenye.

15   Apmer-arenye artnweng-eynenge *school*-we apeyaytenke.

Dialogue 5   *Petrol*-wanenye

Vocabulary

antethenenke	stop	atyerreye	younger brother/sister
apeyakele	nothing	re, repe	he/she/it
eylenke	get	katye	for, on behalf of
akaltye	know	ngkweltye	small change
artnte	rock, hill, money	aweleye	uncle

5.1 Negatives, nothing and being without something

One way to say that you don't have something, or something is lacking, is to use the noun ending **-wanenye**. When this ending is added to a noun the resulting word means 'without' or 'not having' that thing, just as you heard *Petrol*-**wanenye** in dialogue 5, meaning he was out of petrol. This ending may also be used to say that someone or something is not something. For example, adding **-wanenye** to the word **arntwe** 'water' gives **arntwe+wanenye**, which means either 'without water' or 'not water'.

 1   Artweye arelhe-**wanenye**

      man   woman-without

      The man doesn't have a wife

   2   Ayenge mwetekaye-**wanenye**

      I   car-without

      I haven't got a car

3   Re   arntetye-**wanenye**, ahene-rtame

        s/he sick-without   good-CONTRAST

        He's not sick, he's well

Note

Often the ending **-wanenye** is shortened to **-anenye**, without any change in meaning.

5.2   How to say no

The word **apeyakele** can be used as a direct negative answer to a question or request. It can mean 'no', 'nothing', 'no-one' or 'having nothing'. If you want to say that you don't have any of a certain thing, you put the ending +**wanenye** on the thing that you don't have any of, which is then often followed by **apeyakele**. You heard this in dialogue 5 when Thangale said **artnte+wanenye apeyakele** meaning 'no money'.

4   Nge rlwen-akake?

        you   food-having

        Have you got any food?

5   **Apeyakele**

        nothing

        No

6   Re   rlengke alpenkerne?

        s/he today   come back

        Is she coming back today?

7   **Apeyakele**

        nothing

        No

Note

To say 'yes' use either **yewaye**, **yewe**, or **yewe-yewe**.

---

8   Arrwekele apmere atyelarte **apeyakel**arre anenherre

        first   place   at here   nothing+that was

        At first there was nothing here at this place

9   Artnte-**wanenye apeyakele**

money-without   nothing

(I) haven't got any money

10   Artweye arnkenty-arenye   amarlewe **apeyakele**

man   single mens' camp+ORIGIN girl+for   nothing

A man who lives in a single men's camp doesn't have a wife

11   Ngkwarle **apeyakele!**

grog   nothing

No grog!

5.3   How to say you're not doing something

If you want to say that some verb action is not happening, hasn't happened or won't
happen—in other words, turn the verb into the negative—the ending +**nge-wanenye** is
added to the verb. This then translates as 'hasn't', 'isn't', 'didn't', 'can't' or 'couldn't'
do the action. For example **arenge-wanenye** can be translated as: 'will not see', 'does
not see', 'did not see' or 'cannot see'. In dialogue 5 you heard *Petrol*-**eylenge-
wanenye**, meaning 'can't get petrol'.

Note
The ending +**nge-wanenye** does not combine with the tense endings +**nhe**,
+**nke**, +**rantye**, +**ye**, so you can't tell *when* the action didn't take place.

12   Aleke atyeyenge ape**nge-wanenye**

dog   my   go-not

My dog didn't go/isn't going/won't go

13   Atyewe atyeyenge alpe**nge-wanenye**

friend   mine   go-not

My friend didn't go back/isn't going back

14   Atye ngkenge elpathe**nge-wanenye**

I   you   hear-not

I didn't/can't hear you

I didn't/can't understand you

Note
Sometimes people use a shorter form +**ng-anenye** instead of +**nge-wanenye**;
however, both have the same meaning.

15   Atye enye ayne**nge-wanenye**

I   food   eat-not

I haven't had anything to eat

5.4   Telling someone not to do something

To tell someone not to do something in a direct way, like 'don't' in English, the ending +**ntyele** is added to the verb stem.

 16   Rlwene nyarte ayne**ntyelawe**!

food   this   eat+don't+EMPH

Don't eat this food!

17   Atnkwe enwe**ntyele**!

sleep   lie down+don't

Don't go to sleep!

18   Arntwe nyarte kwathe**ntyele**!

water   this   drink+don't

Don't drink this water!

5.5   Kaytetye pronouns

Pronouns are words like 'I', 'you', 'we', 'his' etc. A pronoun doesn't describe the thing it stands for, as a noun does, but simply 'points' to it. In Kaytetye there is no distinction made between male and female in the pronoun system so whereas in English there are three words (he, she, it) which are chosen according to the humanness and the gender of the third party, the word **re** in Kaytetye can refer to a male or a female, or in fact to a thing or an animal.

In English there is one set of pronouns to indicate a single person and another to refer to two or more persons or a group of persons. In Kaytetye there are different sets of *singular*, *dual* and *plural* pronouns, so there are different words for 'I', 'we two' and 'we' (more than two), as there are for 'you', 'you two' and 'you' (more than two), and for 'they', 'those two' and 'those' (more than two).

To make matters more complicated, the form of these pronouns changes depending on which groups of kin are being referred to (or more precisely what relation the people in the group are to each other).

Let's start by taking a look at a table of English pronouns:

Table 2 *English pronouns*

	subject	object	possessive	reflexive
1st person				
singular	I	me	my, mine	myself
plural	we	us	our, ours	ourselves
2nd person				
singular/plural	you	you	your, yours	yourself
3rd person				
singular	he, she, it	him, her, it	his, her, its, hers	herself, himself
plural	they	them	their, theirs	themselves

The columns in table 2 represent the different functions that pronouns have in the sentence ('I' is a *subject*, a doer of an action while 'me' is an *object* or receiver of an action), and the rows show the person ('I', 'he', 'you', etc.) and number of people involved—if there is one person or more than one (plural).

In English and in Kaytetye there are different pronoun forms depending on the function of the pronoun in the sentence. For example, in English we use 'I' for the subject, the one carrying out the action, 'me' for the object, and 'my, mine' for the possessor. It is proper in English to say 'he hit me' rather than 'he hit I'; and 'I hit him' rather than 'me hit he'. The same thing is true in Kaytetye: there are different forms of the pronouns for these different functions. For example:

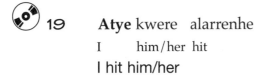 19 **Atye** kwere alarrenhe

       I   him/her hit

       I hit him/her

20 Re **atyenge** alarrenhe

       s/he me   hit

       S/he hit me

21 Re **atyenge** alarrenhe kwerel-arlenge

       s/he me   hit   her/him+in-with

       S/he hit me because of him/her

22 Atye **ngkenge** eylenyerre

       I   to you   got

       I got it for you

23 **Nte** kwere etnye+wethe atewanthe

       You it   give+PURP to them

       You should give it to them

Table 3 lists the singular Kaytetye pronouns and the non-singular pronouns used when the participants are from a different patrimoiety— for example, a group of mothers and children together, or a husband and wife. This set of non-singular pronouns is also used as a kind of 'default' set if the relationships between the people are not known.

Table 3 Kaytetye pronouns (a reduced set)

	subject	object	possessive
1st person			
singular	atye (doer) ayenge	atyenge	atyeyenge
dual exclusive	aylanthe, aylenanthe	aylewanthe, aylekanthe	aylewantheyenge, aylekantheyenge
plural exclusive	aynanthe, aynenanthe	aynewanthe aynekanthe	aynewantheyenge aynekantheyenge
2nd person			
singular	nte (doer) nge	ngkenge	ngkeyenge
dual	mpwelanthe	mpwewanthe	mpwewantheyenge
plural	errwanthe	errwewanthe	errwewantheyenge
3rd person			
singular	re	kwere	kwereyenge
dual	elwanthe	elwewanthe	elwewantheyenge
plural	atanthe	atewanthe	atewantheyenge

Note
See Appendix 5 for a complete set of Kaytetye pronouns.

You can see from table 3 that Kaytetye has many more pronouns than English. In fact English has a very limited pronoun system, which can easily mislead you when you come to learn the Kaytetye pronouns. Although this seems like an awful lot to digest, if you look more closely at table 4 you will start to see patterns emerging in the way the pronouns are made. For example, see how the pronouns in the 'possessive' column have +**yenge** added onto their object form.

There are also slightly different forms of the pronouns depending on whether or not the person being spoken to is included in the group. For example, 'we (including you, the listener)' has a different form of the pronoun from 'we (excluding you, the listener)'.

The pronouns marked in the '*exclusive*' row are the way to say 'a group of us, but excluding you, the person I'm speaking to'.

Possessive pronouns

Listen to the following example sentences which use *possessive pronouns*.

24   Aleke **ngkeyenge** awelengke

     dog   your   dangerous

     Your dog is dangerous

25   Nhartepe   mwetekaye **atyeyenge**

     that+FOCUS   car   mine

     That's my car

The possessive pronouns in Kaytetye aren't always used the same way as the English ones are used. In Kaytetye you don't use possessive pronouns to talk about parts of the body, as they are considered part of you rather than something you own. For example it is more common to say **eltye** *ayenge* 'my hand' rather than **eltye** *atyeyenge* . To say 'my arm', 'leg', 'head' or any body part, the subject or object pronoun is used (**ayenge** 'I', **nge** 'you' and **re** 'he/she/it') instead of **atyeyenge**, **ngkeyenge**, **kwereyenge**. So literally one says 'He hit me arm' or 'I arm ache'.

26   Aleme   ayenge artnweyenteyane

     stomach   I   hurting

     My stomach is hurting

27   Etne   re   Michael

     name   he   Michael

     His name is Michael

28   Tyarlenye ayenge arntenherre

     arm   I   broke

     I broke my arm

Possessive kinship pronouns

The possessive pronouns above are not always used for talking about kin relations, as they are not really things you own. To say 'his/your auntie', 'uncle', 'mother' or any kinship noun, you use a prefix on the start of the kinship word, as in the following examples.

     ngke+   your
     kwe+   his/her/its

To say 'my' relative (cousin, uncle etc.) +**ye** is put onto the end of the kinship noun and the normal possessive pronoun **atyeyenge** is used. This is the possessive pronoun you heard in dialogue 5, as in **aweleye-rtame atyeyenge** '*my* uncle'. Listen and practise saying the following possessive kinship nouns. These pronouns are also used when talking about an animal's 'relations', such as its mother or father.

29   **ngk**awele   your uncle

       kwawele   his/her uncle

       awele**ye** (atyeyenge)   my uncle

30	**ngk**atnkele	your cousin
	kwatnkele	his cousin
	atnkele**ye** (atyeyenge)	my cousin

31   Re apereynenye **kw**empwerne tyangkwerre

       s/he/it took   her+spouse   this way

       She took her husband away with her

32   Re   apenhe **kw**ayletye-ketye   twepe-twepe

       s/he/it went   his+mother-in-law-fear of   around

       He went a long way around to avoid his mother-in-law

If the relation is to more than one person, for example 'our aunt', 'their grandfather', then a different construction is used. This consists of the relation preceded by the object form of the pronoun (see appendix 5).

33   **aylewe** arlweye   the father of us two

34   **mpwewanthe** atnkele   the aunt of you two

35   **atewanthe** arrenge   the grandfather of them

Further information

Some people do use the possessive pronouns when talking about relations, or when talking about body parts, such as **atnkeleye ngkeyenge** 'your aunt', or **atyerreye ayleweyenge** 'the younger sibling of us two'; however, this is more a feature of younger speakers.

'Missing' pronouns

You might have noticed that in the dialogues the words for 'I', **ayenge** and **atye**, are sometimes left out. It is quite common in Kaytetye to leave out the pronoun if it refers to something or someone already mentioned. Although the missing pronoun can be any person or thing, it most often refers to 'he', 'she', 'it', 'they' or 'them'. Listen to the following sentences, where again there is no pronoun corresponding to the English pronoun which is in brackets ('he', 'him', 'she').

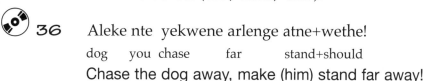

36   Aleke nte   yekwene arlenge atne+wethe!

       dog   you chase   far   stand+should

       Chase the dog away, make (him) stand far away!

37   Artntepe,   akelye   eletnhenke

       stone+FOCUS little   throws

       (He) throws a stone, a little one

38 Errtyewene+le rntwenke weye
teeth+with   cuts   meat
(He) bites the meat with his teeth

39 Nhartepe kwere akwerrarlelke   arrenke
then+FOCUS it   coolamon+to+then puts
Then (she) puts it into a coolamon

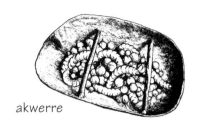
akwerre

5.6   Adding emphasis and contrast

The ending **-rtame** can go on both verbs and nouns and is very common in Kaytetye.
In English, we stress a word to *emphasise* something or contrast two things, whereas in
Kaytetye speakers use **-rtame**. **-rtame** usually goes on the first word of the sentence,
which is usually before the pronoun.

40 Alethange-**rtame** re
stranger-EMPH   he
He's a stranger

41 Akelye-**rtame** re
small-EMPH   it
It's small

42 Aynenge-wanenye-**rtame** re, kwetange tyekerte!
eat-not-EMPH   it plains rat   sour
You can't eat it, the plains rat doesn't taste good!

43 Akaltyele-**rtame**   atye eletnhe+mere
knowledgeable+DOER-EMPH   I   throw+CAN
I know how to throw (a boomerang)

kayle

44 Nthakenhe-**rtame** (nte) mpwarerrantye errtyartepe?
how-EMPH   you making   spear+FOCUS
How do you make a spear?

5.7   Making comparisons

Using **-rtame**

The ending **-rtame** can show that one thing is greater in terms of quantity or quality
than another thing. In English we use the word 'more' or the endings '-er', '-ish', or '-
est' to compare or contrast things: 'bigger', 'biggest', 'smaller', 'smallest'.

-rtame can also be used where English speakers might use 'but', 'however', 'whereas'
and 'than'. **-ketye** can be used on the item that something is being compared to.

45 Errtyarte nhartepe   kngwerepe arreylpe-**rtame**, kngwerepe ametye-**rtame**
spear   that+FOCUS other+FOCUS sharp-CONTRAST   other+FOCUS blunt-CONTRAST
That spear is sharp, the other one is blunter

46 Enye ahene malangke rntwenke, tyekertepe mentye-**rtame**

food good tasty   pick   sour+FOCUS leave-CONTRAST

The good fruits are picked, whereas the rotten, useless ones are left

47 Repe   alkenhe-**rtame**, ayengepe akelye-**rtame**

s/he+FOCUS big-CONTRAST   I+FOCUS   small-CONTRAST

He's older than me

48 Alkemarlayte akepe   alkenhe-**rtame**, atnaympepe akelye-**rtame**

desert poplar grub head+FOCUS big-CONTRAST   bottom+FOCUS small-CONTRAST

The heads of the desert poplar grubs are thicker than their bottoms

Using +*watye*

Another way of comparing things is to use the ending +**watye**. It is a bit like the 'ish' ending in English, as in 'smallish'. It is glossed COMP for comparative.

49

errpwerle	black	errpwerle**watye**	dark complexioned
alkenhe	big	alkenhe**watye**	bigger
errpatye	bad	errpatye**watye**	worse
kwene	deep	kwene**watye**	deeper
ahene	good	ahene**watye**	better

50 Kwelharre   areyneng-apenye akelye**watye**-**rtame** re

black footed rock wallaby euro-like   small+COMP-CONTRAST it

The black-footed rock wallaby is like a euro but smaller

kwelharre

51 Arlkarle**watye** aynanthe elye altyarrenke aherrke-ketye

cold+COMP   we   shade cover   sun-fear of

We'll build a shelter against the heat while it is still cold

Test your skill 5

Listen to dialogue 5 again. Write down the Kaytetye, and an English translation for it.

The following noun phrases need a possessive pronoun in English. In Kaytetye, however, they require different kinds of possessive pronouns; or, for some, none at all. Translate them into Kaytetye.

my dog	_____
your mother	_____
my cousin	_____
his meat	_____
your father	_____
my head	_____
his uncle	_____
her arm	_____

 Listen to these Kaytetye sentences on the CD and repeat them to yourself. Try to work out their meaning in English.

1 Ayenge weye-wanenye apeyakele.
2 Repe artnte+wanenye apeyakele.
3 Repe artnwenge-wanenye.
4 Ngepe aleke-wanenye.
5 Ayenge atyerreye-wanenye.
6 Repe arntetye-wanenye, ahene-rtame.
7 Artnwenge+le aylpatye kwathenge-wanenye.
8 Aleke atyeyenge+le aynenge-wanenye.
9 Mwetekaye antethenenge-wanenye, akanpere apenke.
10 Aynanthe weye atewanthe etnyeye.
11 Atye weye atewanthe etnyeye.
12 Mpwelake atyenge weye etnyeye.

Dialogue 6 Nthekelarte ngepe anteyane?

Vocabulary

Ankweleyelengkwe	place name	etne	name
arrenentye	how many	tyampe	and
arrtyerrantye	look after, hold	ngk+atyerre	your younger sibling
		ntharenyarte	from there
aynanthe	we	nthekelarte?	where at?
atherrarte	two	eleweyenge	their

Further information

The ending +**lengkwe** is often used in place names and things meaning 'characterised by, or having, that thing'. For example, Ankweleyelengkwe, which is a place south-west of Barrow Creek, literally means 'place having wild plums': **ankweleye** (*Santalum lanceolatum*) +**lengkwe**. The animal **atnhelengkwe** 'emu' literally means 'having down/feathers'.

When talking about people's names and country it is common to hear older Kaytetye people using the pronoun **nhante** 'who' and not **wante** 'what', so instead of hearing **etnepe wante-rtame** 'what is his name', you might hear **etnepe nhante-rtame** 'who is his name'.

ankweleye

6.1 Locations and instruments: 'in', 'at', 'on', 'with', 'by'

We have already seen how +**le** and +**nge** are used to show the doer in a transitive sentence. +**le** and +**nge** can also be used to show the location of something, or where an action is happening, particularly in sentences with stance verbs such as **anenke** 'sit', **atnenke** 'stand' and **entwenke** 'lie'. In dialogue 6 you heard +**le** used in this way after the place name Ankweleyelengkwe, meaning 'at Ankweleyelengkwe'. When it is used in this way it may be translated as 'in', 'on', 'at', or 'around'. This ending goes on nouns.

1   Awerre elye**nge** anteyane

      boy   shade+in sitting

      The boy is sitting in the shade

2   Artweye artnte**nge** atnteyane

      man   rock+on   standing

      The man is standing on the rock

Note

For longer words, that is, words with more than one consonant or consonant cluster, +**le** instead of +**nge** is used to mean 'in', 'on', 'at' etc.

3 Arelhe aherrke**le** entweyane

woman   sun+in   lying

The woman is lying in the sun

4 Aleke entweyane apmere**le**

dog   lying   camp+in

The dog is lying in the camp

+**le** and +**nge** can also be used to show the *instrument*, or the thing the action is done with, as can be seen in the following example. It may be translated as 'with (something)' or 'using (something)'.

5 Atye werrantye   aleke artnte**nge**

I   hit by throwing   dog   rock+with

I am hitting the dog with a rock

6 Re ware   eltewenke elepe**le**

s/he firewood splits   axe+with

She splits the firewood with an axe

+**le** and +**nge** can also be used to mark the day, time or season in which an event took place.

7 Atnkwarenge**le** re   alpenherre

night+in   s/he returned

He returned at night

+**le** and +**nge** can also be used to mark things like points in time, particularly on words borrowed from English such as the names of days, months, years etc. They can also be used to mark the means of transport, such as 'by car', 'by plane'.

8 Ayenge apenke Sunday-**le**

I   go   Sunday-on

I'm going on Sunday

9 Mwetekaye**le** ayenge apenke

car+with   I   go

I'm going by car

10 Nantewe**le** ayenge apenke

horse+with   I   go

I'm going by horse

Note

There are certain means of transport which can take a different ending instead of +**le**/+**nge**, or no ending at all.

Ngwetyanpe marnte**l-arlenge** ayenge alpeyerre

tomorrow · bus+in-with · I · return+will

Tomorrow I will go back on the bus

Awatnkakerre aynanthe angketye apeyayne

a long time ago · we · foot · walk+used to

A long time ago we used to travel on foot

Further information

Marnte is an Anmatyerr word meaning 'closed', 'shut' and is used in many Arandic languages to mean 'bus'.

6.2 More on 'this/here' and 'that/there' [demonstratives]

In section 2.1 we saw how to say 'this/here' and 'that/there'. These kinds of words are called *demonstratives*. In dialogue 6 you heard another demonstrative, **ntharenyarte** meaning 'come from there'. If we want to combine a noun ending, such as +**arenye**, +**le**, -**warle**, +**we**, -**penhe**, etc. with a demonstrative—for example to say 'for this one', 'from there', 'to here', etc.—then the following words are used:

Table 4   Some Kaytetye demonstratives

	this / here	that / there
+**we** for	tye**warte** for this	nthe**warte** for that
+**le** on, at, with	tye**larte** on this	nthe**larte** on that
-**angkwerre** through	tya**ngkwerr**arte through here	ntha**ngkwerr**arte through there
-**penhe** after, from	tye**penh**arte from this	nthe**penh**arte from there
-**arenye** belonging to	tya**reny**arte come from here	ntha**reny**arte come from there
-**warle** to	tye**warl**arte to here	nthe**warl**arte to there

Note how the noun ending sits in between the **ty**/**nth** and +**arte** part of the word. The ending +**arte** is also commonly used in question words, such as **wantarte?** 'what's up?'. +**arte** is glossed DEM for demonstrative. It also occurs on number words, such as **atherrarte** 'two' (as you heard in dialogue 6), and with **kwere** 'him/she/it', as in **kwere-penharte** 'after that'. Listen to the following examples which use some of the demonstratives from table 4 above.

 11 **Weye nthewarte** ayenge ahentye anteyane

       meat   for that   I   throat   sitting

       I want that meat

12 **Tyarenyarte** aynanthe arwengerrpe aynterantye

       from here   we   bush turkey   eat

       We eat bush turkeys from around here

13 **Tyarlarte** wampere arwelarle atnywenye

       to here   possum   tree+to   entered

       Right here the possum went into the tree

14 **Nthewarlarte** re weye eletnhenke

       to there   he   meat   puts down

       He puts the animal there

Further information

There are many more demonstratives in Kaytetye than in English. Some others include:

nhakarte	around here
arrenye	over there (distant)
arrewethe, arretyele	that over there
nyaperte	right here
renharte	that one (*the thing previously mentioned*)

6.3 How to say that an action is still happening [present continuous]

In section 1.4 we learnt one way of saying that an action happens now, by using the present tense ending +**nke** on the verb. If the action is more of a state of affairs, or is an action still in progress, you use the ending +**rrane**. This type of present tense is called the *present continuous*. It can sometimes be translated as the '-ing' form of the verb in English, for example in sentences such as 'He is walking', but it also translates as the present tense in English when it refers to things that habitually occur, as in 'snakes live in holes'. This ending is also used to describe feelings, such as 'I am happy'. Listen to the following Kaytetye examples:

15 **Artwey-eynenge** ape**rrane**

       man-lots   going

       All the men are going

16   Weye aherre ampe**rrane**

   meat   kangaroo cooking

   The kangaroo is cooking

17   Mpwenyelpe (re)   antye**rrane** eylkwenng-apenye

   mpwenyelpe   s/he   jumping   mouse-like

   The *mpwenyelpe (type of mouse)* jumps like a mouse

18   Aleme ayenge aterarre**rane**

   stomach I   frightened

   I'm frightened

Not all verbs take the +**rrane** ending to show the incomplete present tense. There are three different endings and the type of verb will determine which ending the verb takes. Most verbs take the ending +**rrane** as we saw above; however, verbs that have **n** or **nw** in the stem before the ending take +**yane**. You also need to insert a **t** after the **n** in the verb stem, as in examples 19–20 below. The inserted **t** is the underlined letter. You heard a verb with this ending in dialogue 6, **anteyane**. This is the most common way of saying something is or lives at a certain place.

19   Aynanthe an<u>t</u>e**yane**

   We   sitting

   We are sitting down (**anenke** 'sits')

20   Elyenge re atn<u>t</u>e**yane**

   shade+in he sitting

   He is standing in the shade (**atnenke** 'stands')

21   Artarrarle eyteye en<u>t</u>we**yane**

   Artarre+to   road   lying

   The road goes to Artarre (**enwenke** 'lies')

These verbs often describe a position or stance, whereas the +**rrane** verbs often describe types of movement, emotions and states of affairs.

The third type of verb takes the ending +**rrantye** for the present continuous. The verbs that take this ending are all transitive, that is, they require a 'doer'. In section 4.5 transitive and intransitive verbs were discussed. You might want to go back to page 59 to brush up on what this means. The present continuous tense is +**rrantye** for transitive verbs, and +**rrane** or +**yane** for intransitive verbs.

Luckily for the Kaytetye learner, the present continuous tense is the only verb tense that changes its form depending on whether the verb is transitive, intransitive or has a 'n/nw' in its stem.

22   Artweyele aleke alarre**rantye**

   man+DOER   dog   hitting

   The man is hitting the dog

23   Artweyele atnwenthe aynte**rantye**

man+DOER   meat   eating

The man is eating meat

24   Artnwengele artweye are**rrantye**

child+DOER   man   looking

The child is looking at the man

Note

The ending +**rrane** becomes +**rane**, and +**rrantye** becomes +**rantye** if the verb has any of the sounds (before the verb ending) in columns 3–5 on page 10:

25

pwe**rrantye**	cooking	aynte**rantye**	eating
ange**rrantye**	digging	ayle**rantye**	singing
etye**rrantye**	put up	alarre**rantye**	hitting
eye**rrantye**	grinding	arre**rantye**	putting
are**rrantye**	seeing	rntwe**rantye**	picking, cutting
ape**rrane**	going	ertwe**rane**	going down
angke**rrane**	speaking	ayte**rane**	coming up
antye**rrane**	jumps	kengkarre**rane**	sneaking up on

Listen to dialogue 6 again and pick out the four times a verb in the present continuous tense occurs.

6.4   How to say that an action goes on for a long time

To say that an action goes on for a long time, or it keeps happening, you use the ending **-ee** after the tense. This ending can go on any tense. In speech the **-ee** can be extended for quite some time, showing that the action happened for a really long time. It is often translated as 'kept on' or 'for a long time'.

26   Nthethey-aperte alpenherre-**ee**   atwerrpep-aperte

from there-just   returned+CONTINUE afternoon+FOCUS-just

From there they kept coming this way and in the afternoon they stopped

27   Elyengepe   atanthepe pweyayne-**ee**

shade+in+FOCUS   they+FOCUS   cook+used to-CONTINUE

They would cook (the meat) in the shade for a long time

28   Angketyelke ayleme apenhe-ngerne-**ee**

foot+now   we two   went-this way-CONTINUE

We kept walking, coming this way

6.5 'there is', 'there are'

By using the verb ending +**yane** on the verb **anenke** 'sit' it is possible to say 'there is' or 'there are'. You can change the meaning to 'there was', 'there will be' or 'there used to be' by using a different tense ending on the verb:

+nhe   there was
+ye   there will be
+yayne   there used to be

 29   *Meeting* ante**yane**

          meeting   sitting

          There is a meeting

makwele

     30   Eyterrtye makwele ante**yane**

          people   many   sitting

          There are lots of people

     31   Alewenpe anthwerrke ante**yane**

          lots of   unripe   sitting

          There are lots of unripe ones

     32   Thangkenharengele makwele kwelharre   etnteyele ante**yane**

          Barrow Creek+at   lots   black footed rock wallabies   caves+in   sitting

          At Barrow Creek there are lots of black footed rock wallabies in the caves

     33   Anatye ayerrere makwele ante**yane**

          Yams   north   lots   sitting

          There are lots of yams to the north

As well as 'sit', some other types of stance verbs are used to say 'there is'. For example, to say 'There is water in the creek' the verb for 'lying' must be used. That is, roads and creeks all 'lie'; they don't sit and so you must use **entweyane** 'lying'. For trees, other plants and cars the verb for 'standing' **atnteyane** must be used. For houses, hills and some other geographical features the verb for 'crouching', **altyanteyane**, must be used.

If you want to say 'there was', 'there were' the verb is put in the past tense.

 34   Arntwe elpayele entwe**yane**

          water   creek+in   lying

          There is water in the creek

     35   Arwele alkenhe atnte**yane**

          tree   big   standing

          There is a big tree

     36   Twerrp-amerne akngerrake altyante**yane**

          sandhill+PLURAL   east   crouching

          There are sandhills in the east

37   Artnte altyante**yane** Atyertepentye

 hill crouching Atyertepentye

 The hill there is Atyertepentye (Watt Range)

38   Arntwe enwe**nherre** elpayele

 water lay   creek+in

 There was water in the creek

39   Eyerrtye makwele ane**nherre**

 people many sat

 There were lots of people

6.6 Ways to join words together: 'and', 'too', 'as well'

The word 'and' is used frequently in the English language. In Kaytetye there are several different ways of linking things together in a sentence in a way that would translate into English as 'and'.

One way of joining words together in a sentence is by simply listing them, one after the other, with a pause in between:

40   Kwementyaye Mary kwenyele apenhe-ngerne

 Kwementyaye Mary yesterday went-this way

 Kwementyaye and Mary came yesterday

41   Artwey-amerne apenherre aherrewe, atnhelengkwewe, arwengerrpewe

 man+PLURAL   went kangaroo+for emu+for   bush turkey+for

 The men went for kangaroo, emu and bush turkey

Using **ane**

Another way is to use the word **ane**, which is adapted from the English word 'and'. It can be used to join lists of words together in a sentence and can occur between all the nouns listed or it can be put between the last two nouns of a list.

42   Rlwene atye aynenye, **ane** kayte   atye aynenye

 vegetables I ate   and witchetty grubs I ate

 I ate vegetable food and witchetty grubs

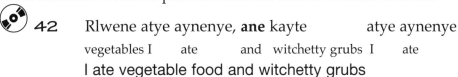

Note

The word **ane** cannot be used to join pronouns. You can't say, for example, **Rosie ane ayenge**.

Using **tyampe, kape**

When joining two things or two groups of things together, particularly pairs of words that commonly occur together such as 'man and woman' or 'tea and sugar', the word

tyampe is used, either after each word, or at the end of the two items, as in this example:

43   Teye tyweke-**tyampe**   tea and sugar
     Teye-**tyampe** tyweke-**tyampe**   tea and sugar

It would be unacceptable to use **tyampe** to join two words that aren't commonly associated with each other such as 'woman' and 'sugar'. (You also heard **tyampe** in dialogue 6 when two brothers were named.)

44   Artweye **tyampe** arelhe   **tyampe** apenherre
     man   and   woman   and   went
     The man and woman went

45   Enyepe   altywerewenherre alekel-eynenge,
     food+FOCUS opened   dog+DOER-lots

     tyweke-tywekel-eynenge **tyampe**
     chook+DOER-lots   and
     The dogs and the chooks opened the food

46   Kngwarraye-**tyamp**-arenge (arelhe) Pwerle-**tyamp**-arenge
     (skin name)-and -'s   (woman)   (skin name)-and-'s

     artnwengepe Kapetye-rtame
     child+FOCUS   (skin name)+EMPH
     A Kngwarraye (man) and a (Pwerle) woman's children are Kapetye

Tyampe is used if you want to say 'too', 'as well', or 'also'.

47   Apenerne   nge **tyampe** erlpewatne+wethe
     go+command+this way   you and   listen+PURP
     Come on over, so you can listen too

Note
Some speakers use the word **kape** instead of **tyampe**.

Beware
Some people pronounce **tyampe** as **tyame**. However, it is still written as **tyampe**.

Using -therre
When two people are being referred to in a sentence and they are commonly thought of as being closely associated in some way, such as close friends, a pair of siblings, or a couple, the names of these people can be joined in a sentence by putting **-therre** after each name. You heard this in dialogue 6 when he said **etnepe-therrepe** meaning 'their two names'.

48   Mary-le**therre** Susie-le**therre** Kaytetyele   akalty-etnye+wethe

Mary+DOER-two Susie+DOER-two Kaytetye+with knowledge-give+PURP

Mary and Susie taught Kaytetye

Sometimes the second name in such a sentence is left out altogether, leaving one name with **-therre** after it, but still meaning that two people were carrying out the verb action. It is assumed that the listener will know who the other person is. So you could say:

 49   Mary-le**therre** Kaytetyele   akalty-etnyewethe

Mary-DOER+two Kaytetye+with knowledge-give+PURP

Mary and the other one (*i.e. Susie*) taught Kaytetye

50   Kwementyaye-**therre**

Kwementyaye and her husband/Kwementyaye and his wife

Further information
We said before that **ane** cannot be used to connect pronouns, and in fact none of the ways listed above of saying 'and' in Kaytetye are used to do this. Something which is quite different from English usage happens when you want to connect a pronoun and a person together. The correct way to say 'Rosie and I' is **Rosie ayleme** (that is if Rosie is your sister or has the same skin name as you).
Other examples:

atyerreye ayleme

brother (my) we two (exclusive)

younger brother and I (*literally: 'brother we two'*)

arlweye aylake

father (my) we two (inclusive)

father and I (*literally: 'father we two'*)

arrengkwe aylenanthe

mother (my) we two (exclusive)

mother and I (*literally: 'mother we two'*)

Further information
It is also possible to say **arrengkwe tyampe aylenanthe** or **arlweye tyampe aylake**.

Note that the pronouns used in these types of constructions must reflect the kin relations between the members of the group. See section 10.6 for more about kin terms.

Using **-nhenge**
The ending **-nhenge** means 'people who are of a certain relationship to each other together'. It goes on the end of kin terms. You can also put **-therre** or **-amerne**, or **-eynenge** after **-nhenge** if you want to specify how many people there are in that relationship to each other. For example:

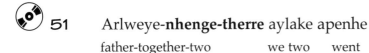

51 Arlweye-**nhenge-therre** aylake apenhe

father-together-two   we two   went

We two, who are related as father and child, went

52 Ayleme alkere-**nhenge-therre** apenherre

we two   brother-together-two   went

We two brothers went

Note

In this section you have learnt how to say 'and' if you are joining things, or nouns. There is a different way to say 'and' if you are talking about doing more than one action. This is discussed in 10.4 on page 116.

Test your skill 6

Listen to dialogue 6 again. Write down the Kaytetye, and an English translation for it.

 Listen to these Kaytetye sentences on the CD and repeat them to yourself. Try to work out their meaning in English.

1   Aleke anteyane elye+nge.

2   Amarle+le angerrantye anatye atneme+le.

3   Artweye-therre+le errtyarte+le aytnenke atnhelengkwe.

4   Ngkwerne+le pwetyerrepe anenke.

5   Wante ntepe mpwarerrantye?

6   Artweye kngwere aytnenke artweye tyelarte.

7   Nthekelarte ngepe anteyane?

8   Awerr-eynenge tyampe kwerr-eynenge tyampe apenkerne.

9   Tyanywenge tyampe arlpe tyampe nte atyenge etnyene!

10   Arrere-nhenge-therre elweme anatye+we aperrane.

11   Rlwene *bush*-arenyepe ahene-rtame rlwene rlwamp-arenge-ketye.

12   Errpwerle+watye-rtame nhartepe.

13   Errpwerle+watye-rtame nhartepe, nyarte amelh-amelhe-rtame.

14   Arlkerre erreyakwerre atye karntape-warle arrenhe.

15   Aleke artnperrane atnkwarengele.

16   Artweye+le aleke alarrenhe arwele+le.

17   Ayenge aleke atyeyenge tyampe *shop*-warle apenhe.

Dialogue 7   Aleme ayenge ngayele

Vocabulary

ahene	good	aynenke	eat
akeleye	(my) aunt (father's sister)	eylenke	get
		ekwe malangke	tasty, delicious
aleme	stomach, liver	mpele	thus, like that
alepetyenke	taste, try	ngayele	hungry
alewatyerre	goanna	nthakenhe	how
alhwenge	hole	pwenke	cook
apmerrke	hot coals	weye	meat
nthakenhe	how	aweparenke	wait

Further information

Akeleye is the word for father's sisters; it does not apply to mother's sisters, these are called **arrengkwe** 'mother'. Similarly, **aweleye** 'uncle' only applies to your mother's brothers. Your father's brothers are called **arlweye** 'father'.

7.1   How to say something is similar to something else

The ending **-apenye** shows that something is similar to, or like, something else. This ending goes on nouns. Listen to the following examples.

1   nth**apeny**arte
     like that one

2   ty**apeny**arte
     like this one

3   want-**apenye**?
     what-like
     like what/what's it like?

4   Rlwene atyeyenge artnt**apenye**
     food   my   rock+like
     My damper is like a stone

Note

Some people say **nyart-apenye** instead of **tyapenyarte**, but they mean the same thing. Other demonstratives can also be formed by adding the ending to **nyarte** and **nharte** in this way.

7.2 'with', 'having': -akake

When **-akake** is added to a word the resulting word means 'someone/something having that thing', in the sense of having it with them, but not necessarily owning it. **-akake** may be translated as 'with', 'having' or 'holding' something. In dialogue 7 you heard **atnwenthe rlwene-tyamp-akake nge** 'have you got any tucker or meat?'

5　Artweye arrkar-**akake**

man　　spouse-having

The man is married

6　Ngepe　arntw**akake**

you+FOCUS　water+having

You've got water

7　Re arntety-akake

s/he sickness-having

S/he is sick (*having sickness*)

7.3 'from': -theye

There are many uses of the word 'from' in English, for example: 'I come from Sydney', 'I came from the bank', 'Milk comes from cows'. In Kaytetye there are a number of endings which correspond to these meanings of the English word 'from', and one of these is **-theye**.

The ending **-theye** shows where someone or something moves from, or is moved from, or where someone or something has just come from. You heard **alhwenge-theye** 'from a hole' in dialogue 7. **-theye** can also show the reason for something happening. It can be translated as 'away from', 'from', or 'off'.

8　Ntheke-**they**arte

where-from+DEM

Where from?

9　Arelhe Alekarenge-**theye** apenhe-ngerne

woman　Alekarenge-from　　came-this way

The woman just came from Alekarenge

10　Eylpe ahenele　arlenge-**theye** elpatherrantye

ear　　good+with　far-from　　　　hearing

With my good ears I can hear from a long distance

11　Elhe**theye** nge arrknge erretarrenke (nge)

nose+from　you　blood　flows　　　you

Your nose is bleeding

Note

Remember endings on short words don't have hyphens.

-theye can mean 'of' or 'from' in the sense of 'north of', 'south of', 'this side of'. **-theye** goes on the object word and not the direction word.

12   Apmere Apewempe ayerrere Thangkenharenge-**theye**

      place   Apewempe   north   Thangkenharenge-from

      Taylor's Crossing is north of Barrow Creek

-theye is also used to mean 'in' or 'into' in the sense of: translate something into, or speak in a language.

13   Ngerteye   Kaytetye-**theye** atnawerreyne+wethe?

      you+UNCERTAIN Kaytetye-from   turn over/translate+PURP

      Can you translate it into Kaytetye?

7.4   'should', 'intend to', 'ought': +**wethe**

The ending +**wethe** is used if the action should happen, or if there is an intention to do the action. It goes on the end of verbs and is glossed PURP, which is short for purposive. It can also be used in the sense of 'want to' do something.

14   Elyenge ayenge ane**wethe**

      shade+in I   sit+PURP

      I'm going to sit in the shade

15   Aynanthe apmere kngwere-warlelke ape**wethe**

      we   camp   another-to+now   go+PURP

      We'll go to another place now

16   Ngayele ayenge, weye atye ayne**wethe**

      hungry I   meat I   eat+PURP

      I'm hungry, I want to eat some meat

In the case of sentences with two verbs, +**wethe** shows that something is done for a purpose, that is, 'in order to do something else' or 'so that something else can happen'. This often translates as 'to do such and such' in English.

17   Ayenge elpaye-warle ape**wethe** arntwe atye eyle**wethe**

      I   creek-to   go+PURP   water I   get+PURP

      I'm going to the creek to get water

18   Anewene atyengel-arlenge, aleme   atyenge ahen+eyne**wethe**

      sit+MUST me+in-with   stomach me   good+make+PURP

      Stay with me, to make me feel good

The ending +**wethe** can also go after the imperfect tense (these are the endings +**rrane**, +**rrantye** and +**yane** which you learnt about in section 6.3). When +**wethe** comes after one of these endings it means 'in order to keep doing something' or 'in order to do something for a while'.

19 Ayenge apenke ane**wethe**

I go sit+PURP

I'm going to sit down

20 Ayenge apenke anteyane**wethe**

I go sitting+PURP

I'm going to stay for a while

21 Alpereynenkelke kwere, apmere-warle, aynterantye**wethe**

take back+now it camp-to eating+PURP

Then (he) takes it back to camp to continue eating it

22 Arlelke ape**wethe**!

hunting go+PURP

Let's go hunting!

23 Arlelke aperrane**wethe**!

hunting going+PURP

We should continue hunting

7.5 'again', 'as well', 'more': -apertame

To ask for more of something, or say that you want to do something again you use the ending **-apertame** on the verb, just as you heard in dialogue 7: **etnyewen-apertame atyenge**! 'give me some more!'. Notice how **-apertame** comes *after* the tense marking on the verb. This ending can also go on nouns. In this case it means 'as well' or 'too'.

24 Angken-**apertame** nge!

talk-again you

Say it again!

25 Aynen-**apertame** nte!

eat-again you

Eat some more!

26 Arwele kwere akelye-**apertame**

stick it small-again

rntwey-**apertame** kwere

will cut-again it

He will cut a small stick for it too

pwenke

27 Eylerakwe pwenke aherr-apeny-**apertame**

spectacled hare wallaby cook kangaroo-like-again

You cook the spectacled hare-wallaby like a kangaroo as well

7.6 'thus', 'really': **mpele**

The word **mpele** translates as 'thus', 'like this', 'in this way' or 'hey', or sometimes it just adds emphasis to what someone is saying, as in dialogue 7 where you heard '**ekwe malangke, ahene mpele!**'—'it's *really* tasty!'.

 28   Arntwe nyartepe tyekerte **mpele**!

    water   this+FOCUS salty   thus

    Hey, this water is *really* salty!

29   Atyarlarte re arwelarle atnywenye **mpele**!

    in here+DEM it tree+in   entered   thus

    Oh, *right here* it went into a tree!

The frequently used Kaytetye word **mpelarte** is based on this word. **Mpelarte** can be both a question and an answer:

30   **Mpelarte**?

    Like this?

31   Yewe, **mpelarte**

    Yes, like that

Test your skill 7

Listen to dialogue 7 again. Write down the Kaytetye, and an English translation for it.

Listen to these Kaytetye sentences on the CD and repeat them to yourself. Work out their meaning in English.

1   Rlwene nharte want-apenye?

2   Enye atyenge eylene nte nthapenyarte!

3   Re apenke apmere-theye.

4   Elpaye-warle ayenge apenke arntwe eylewethe.

5   Awerre nharte mwekart-akake.

6   Artnwenge alek-akake.

7   Ayneweth-apertame nte!

8   Weye atye aynewethe.

9   Ahene aynanthe akngke angkewethe.

10   Weye atye aynterantyewethe.

11   Arlelke aynanthe apewethe.

12   Arlelke aynanthe aperranewethe.

13   Arlelke apen-apertame errwanthe!

14   Rlwene nyarte ekwe malangke mpele!

15   Aleke artnperrane apmere-theye.

16   Aylanthe elye+nge anewethe arlkarl+arrewethe.

Dialogue 8   *Store*-warle apewethe

Vocabulary

ahentye	throat	mwetekaye	car
amarle	girl	ngkertarrenke	be naughty
arlkeny-arlkenye	stripy	tywekere	dislike
kwenyele	yesterday	akelye	small
mame	mum	alkenhe	big, lots of
mantarre	clothes	nthewarte	for that (one)
mentye	leave it		

8.1   How to say something is owned by someone

The ending -**arenge** is like the apostrophe **s** in English: it expresses ownership, as in
'the girl's dog'. It can also be translated as 'belonging to'. You heard it in dialogue 8:
mantarre amarle-arenge meaning 'women's clothes'. It may be added to nouns to
show that a person or thing belongs to the noun with -**arenge**. Notice how the person
or thing that is owned may come after (as in example 1) or before (as in example 2) the
noun with -**arenge** ending.

 1   Arelh-**arenge** atnwenthe

   woman-'s   meat

   The woman's meat

2   Aleke nyarte artwey-**arenge**

   dog   this   man's

   This is the man's dog

Sometimes it is difficult to understand when to use -**arenge** and when to use -**akake**.
Listen to the following examples that use both -**arenge** and -**akake**. Try to work out the
type of situations where to use -**arenge** and where it is correct to use -**akake**.

   Nge arelh-**arenge** atnem-**akake**

   you woman's   digging stick-having

   You've got the woman's digging stick

But if you were referring to your digging stick:

   Arelhe atneme   ngkeyeng-**akake**

   woman digging stick yours-having

   The woman has got your digging stick

   Atneme   ngkeyeng-**akake** nge

   digging stick yours-having   you

   You've got your digging stick

atneme

Further information

There are many place names and words for things that are made up from this ending, for example:

Alekarenge	place name (**aleke** 'dog')
erlwarenge	glasses (**erlwe** 'eye')
etntyarenge	comb (**etntye** 'hair')
atnkwarengele	night-time (**atnkwe** 'sleep')

When you are talking about owners or people responsible for a particular country or Dreamings, or about people closely associated with a place or thing, the ending **-artweye** or **-arteye** goes on the country or Dreaming. This ending is always preceded by the +**we** ending (the *dative* ending, which we saw in section 3.2).

apmerew-**artwey**-amerne

country-for-ASSOC+PLURAL

'owners' of a country

aherrew-**artey**-amerne

kangaroo-for-ASSOC+PLURAL

people responsible for kangaroo/Kangaroo Dreaming people

Tnhante nthew**artwey**arte?

Who   that one+ASSOC

Who is the owner of that country?

It is important to note that the concepts of ownership expressed by the use of these words are very difficult to translate into English.

8.2 How to say something has already happened

To say that an action happened, that is, put it in the past tense, the ending +**nhe** is used. However, this ending becomes +**nye** if there is a **y** in the preceding consonant.

Note

In section 3.4 you learnt that the verb **apenkerne** 'come' has an irregular future tense ending (**aperrernenyeye**). The past tense of this verb is also irregular: **apenhe-ngerne** 'came' and not **apenherne**.

artweye apenkerne	the man comes
artweye apenhe-ngerne	the man came
artweye aperrernenyeye	the man will come

 3   Artweye nharte ape**nhe**rre

man   that   went

That man went

4   Atnyemayte atye ayne**nye**

witchetty grubs I   ate

I ate witchetty grubs

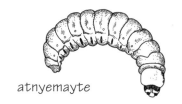

atnyemayte

Note

Some people make the verb a bit longer when they talk by putting +**rre** on the end of the past tense verb, so **enwenhe** becomes **enwenherre**, and **anenhe** becomes **anenherre**. This also happens to the future tense of the verb +**ye**, as you saw in section 3.4. These are the only two tenses where this happens.

8.3   How to say that you want or like something

You may have noticed example 11 in chapter 6, which literally says 'I'm throat sitting for that meat.' To say that you want, feel like having, desire or like something or someone, you use the phrase **ahentye anenke**, which means 'throat sit'. The verb **anenke** can be put in any tense, as you do for any other verb, so 'I want*ed*' (past tense) is **ayenge ahentye ane*nhe***.

If it is an action that is wanted, then the verb takes the PURP ending +**wethe** (see section 7.4). If it is a thing that is wanted or liked, then the noun takes the dative ending +**we**. In dialogue 8 you heard the child say **ahentye anteyane** 'want' and **nthewarte** 'that one', when she saw things in the shop that she wanted.

5   **Ahentye anenke** ayenge ane**wethe**

throat   sits   I   sit+PURP

I want to go and sit down

6   Weye**we** ayenge **ahentye anteyane**

food+for I   throat   sitting

I want some meat

7   Ayenge **ahentye anteyane** amarle nthewarte

I   throat   sitting   girl   for that one

I really like that girl

8.4   How to say you don't like or don't want something

To say that you don't like something you use the noun **tywekere** (as you heard the child say in dialogue 8) or **atnkewanenye** meaning 'dislike'. The thing that you dislike takes the dative ending +**we**.

8   Ayenge **tywekere** atnwenthe aylperre**we**

I   dislike   meat   fish+for

I don't like fish

9 Artweye **tywekere** nthamernewartepe (re)

    man   dislike   for those ones   (s/he/it)

The man doesn't want those ones

10 Warenpe nte eylene   ayenge **atnkewanenye** arlkarle-ketye

    hot   you get+COMMAND I   dislike   cold-fear of

Get a warmer one because I don't like cold ones

8.5   'only', 'just' 'exclusively'

When the endings **-aperte** or **-apaperte** are added to a word the meaning is 'right', 'just', 'only', 'still' or 'entirely that thing'. You heard this in dialogue 8 when the mother said she only had enough money for food. These endings can go on both verbs and nouns. Sometimes the word **ape** is also heard on its own, to mean 'a bit' or 'just'. Listen to the following examples.

11 Ny**apertawe**!

    here+just+hey

It's here!

12 Ny**aperte** atnywenyawe!

    here+just   entered+hey

It went in right here!

13 Arrwekel-**aperte** (re) ampwarrenhe

    in front-just   it died

Did it die just ahead

14 Ayenge ampw**aperte**

    I   weak+just

I'm still weak

15 Alkaperte **ape** atye ampeylewethe

    OK   just I   tell+PURP

OK, I should just tell a bit

16 **Ape** ayenge angkerrane

    Just I   talking

I'm just talking

8.6   How to ask questions in Kaytetye

It is very important for the language learner to be able to ask questions. There are a number of ways to ask questions in Kaytetye.

One of the simplest ways is to use a different intonation, so a sentence can be turned into a question simply by changing your voice at the end of the sentence. Listen to the following pairs of sentences. In each pair the first sentence is a statement and the second one is a question.

17 Artweye apenherre

man   went

The man went

18 Artweye apenherre?

man   went

Did the man go?

19 Arelhe artnweng-akake

woman   child-having

The woman has a child

20 Arelhe artnweng-akake?

woman   child-having

Does the woman have children?

Question words—[interrogatives]: 'what', 'when', 'why' etc.

Another way of asking questions is to use a question word, such as 'what', 'when', 'why', 'how' in English. Below is a list of Kaytetye question words.

Table 5   Some Kaytetye question words

ntheke / nthekarte	which
nthekele / nthekelarte	where
elewe / elewarte	when
wante / wantarte	what
wantewe / wantewarte	why
nthakenhe	how
arrenentye	how many
tnhante / tnhantarte	who
nthakenharrenke	what's up
nthakenhaylenke	what doing (e.g. *what is s/he doing*)

Remember that noun endings go on these words, just as they do on other nouns, so 'where from?' is **ntheketheye**?, 'scared of what?' is **wanteketye**? etc.

It is common to hear +**arte** on the end of many of these question words, just as it goes on the end of the 'this/that/these/those' words (**nyarte/nharte**). This is glossed DEM for demonstrative (see section 6.2). Listen to the following examples; some of these you have already heard in the dialogues.

21 **Nthek-angkwerre** nge apenhaye?

where-through   you went+hey

Where did you go?

22   **Wantewe** errwanthe arrkantarreranaye?

　　　　what+for　　you all　　　laughing+hey

　　　　Why are you lot laughing?

23   **Wante-penhe** nge akerleyt+arrerane?

　　　　what-from　　　you being quiet+becoming

　　　　Why are you being quiet?

24   **Wante-penhe** nge akepe?

　　　　what-from　　　you head+FOCUS

　　　　What happened to your head?

25   **Tnhantele** ngkenge akalty-etnyenye?

　　　　who+DOER　you　　　knowledge-gave

　　　　Who taught you?

26   **Tnhant-arenge** mwetekayepe arntenhe?

　　　　who-'s　　　　　car+FOCUS　　　broke down

　　　　Whose car broke down?

27   **Tnhantewe** nte enye pwerrantye?

　　　　who+for　　you food　cooking

　　　　Who are you cooking for?

28   **Nthekewe** nte apmwe arenhaye?

　　　　where+for　you snake　saw+hey

　　　　Where did you see the snake?

29   **Elewarte**　　nge　alpeye(rre)?

　　　　when+DEM　　you　go back+will

　　　　When are you going back?

30   **Nthakenhe** nte pwenkepe kwere?

　　　　how　　　　you cook+FOCUS　it

　　　　How do you cook it?

31   Artnwengepe ngkeyenge **arrenentye**?

　　　　child+FOCUS　　　your　　　　how many

　　　　How many children do you have?

~~~~~~

Useful phrase
wantakerrertetye or **wantakertetye** 'all sorts of', 'any sort of'. This is based on
the word **wante** 'what' (**wante+akerre+rtetye**).

~~~~~~

'what about', 'how about...?'

Another way to ask a question is to use the noun ending **-rteye**. This is one of the most common ways to ask a question in Kaytetye. It is used if the speaker is uncertain, and wants to know about something. It was heard in dialogue 8 when the mother said **nyarte-rteye**? 'what about this one?' Sometimes another ending +**ange** is used, which has a similar meaning. Listen to the following examples.

32   Mary-**rteye**?
      Mary-UNCERTAIN
      Where's Mary?/What about Mary?

33   Nge**rteye**   angke+mere Kaytetye?
      you+UNCERTAIN talk+CAN   Kaytetye
      Can you speak Kaytetye?

34   Weye-**rteye**   areynenge?
      meat-UNCERTAIN euro
      Hey, was there any euro?

35   Arlweye-**rteye** nthek-angkwerre apenhe(rre) apmere-warle?
      father-UNCERTAIN whereabouts   went   camp-to
      Which way did your father go to camp?

36   Kwementyayel-**apeke**   kwere   alarrenhe?
      Kwementyaye+DOER-PERHAPS her   hit
      Was it Kwementyaye who hit her?

37   Akngw**ange**   nge?
      mad+UNCERTAIN   you
      Are you mad?

38   Ahen**ange**   atye arerrantye?
      good+UNCERTAIN I   looking
      May I watch?

8.7   More about describing words

In section 2.4 you learnt some nouns that are used to describe things. There are also other Kaytetye words used to describe things that are made by reduplicating whole words or parts of words. These doubled-up words have a slightly different meaning from the original word. The process is quite complicated and it is beyond the scope of this learner's guide to go into it in detail, but here are some interesting examples of this process:

39   atherrke   general term for green plants
      atherrk-atherrke   green

      kngwere   another, other, different
      kngwer-kngwere   one day soon, another time

elpalhe	smoke
elpalh-elpalhe	smoky
aylepe	hairstring
aylep-aylepe	matted, knotty hair
arlkenye	stripe, marking, groove
arlkeny-arlkenye	stripy
ampenye	deserted, empty
ampeny-ampenye	scraps, leftovers
athame	no fire, without light or heat
atham-athame	kind, compassionate
arletye	raw
arlety-arletye	half cooked

Note

As you might have noticed, sometimes the doubled-up words are very different in meaning from the original word, or the connections between the meanings of the two words may not be immediately apparent.

Test your skill 8

Write down the Kaytetye, and an English translation for Dialogue 8.

 Listen to these Kaytetye sentences on the CD and repeat them to yourself. Work out their meaning in English.

1   Nthekelarte ngepe anteyane?

2   Nge+pe apmere nthek-arenye?

3   Artweye alarrenhe nantewe+le.

4   Atye kwenyele alarrenhe wampere.

5   Anatye arrmaly-arrmalye atye aynenyerre.

6   Ntheke-theye ngepe apenhe+ngerne kwenyele?

7   Arntwe errpatye kwathentyele!

8   Anene nge, artnperrayte+ntyele!

9   Ahentye anteyane ayenge, weye aynewethe.

10   Ayenge ahentye anteyane amarle nthewarte.

11   Tyangkwerrartep+ange *store*-warlepe?

12   Ahen+ange ayenge apeme errwanthe+l-arlenge?

Turn the following sentences into questions.

1   Ayenge elpaye-warle apenke.

Nthekewarlarte ngepe apenke?

2   Atnwenthe atye aynterantye.

_____

3   Atyerreye atherrarte atyeyenge.

_____

4   Arlelke repe apenke weye+we.

_____

5   Ayenge arntetye ngkwarle-penhe.

_____

6   *Barrow Creek*-le ayenge anteyane.

_____

7   Kwenyele atanthe apenherre.

_____

8   Elye aynanthe mpwarerrantye.

_____

Dialogue 9   Arntetyarreme-ketye

aherne	dirt	eltye	hand
anenke	sit	errkweyenenke	go and wash
arenke	see, look	eylatnenke	play
arntety-arrenke	get sick	mpwelanthe	you two
artennge	dirty	ntewenhe	yourself
aylewenhanthe	ourselves	nthakenharrenke?	what's happening?
elpere	quick		

9.1 'because of', 'lest', 'in case'

The ending **-ketye** can go on the end of verbs or nouns to show that something is disliked, feared, or may have unwanted consequences unless the suggested action is undertaken. On nouns it can go on the end of something that people feel negatively about. It is often translated as 'because of', 'from', 'lest', 'for fear of', 'in case' or 'away from'.

1 Apmwe**ketye**awe!

snake+fear of+hey

Watch out for snakes!

2 Eyteye-**ketye** nge apenawe!

road-fear of   you   go+hey

Move out of the way!

3 Aleke artnperraytenye nantewe-**ketye**

dog   ran away   horse-fear of

The dog ran away from the horse

4 Artweyele antywe mpwarerrantye arntwe**ketye**

man+DOER   humpy making   water+fear of

The man is making a humpy as protection from the rain

Note

-ketye can also be used in the situation where kin avoidances are being referred to:

Artweye re   twaltye-**ketye**   eyntwemel+arrenhe

man   s/he mother-in-law-fear of face away+became

The man faced away from his mother-in-law

In this situation it is not being suggested that his mother-in-law will actually cause him physical harm unless he turns away, but that social conventions and behaviour should be adhered to. For more discussion of this sort of 'avoidance' behaviour see page 124.

9.2 'might', 'could', 'in case': +me-ketye

On verbs **-ketye** shows that an action may have unwanted consequences unless the suggested action is undertaken; that is, something bad might happen. In a sentence where there are two verbs the addition of **-ketye** to one of them indicates that the other action should be carried out in order to avoid the first.

The ending +**ketye** must be preceded by +**me**, or +**mere** when added to a verb stem. See section 10.3 for more about the +**me**/+**mere** ending. In dialogue 9 you heard **arntetyarre+me-ketye,** meaning 'because you might get sick'

5   Nyarte arlwengkeyne**me(re)-ketye**

　　this　　forget+CAN-in case

　　In case you forget this

6   Ayenge tyert-atnywenke, atyeyenge-ketye, alwengaye**me-ketye**

　　I　　hide-go in　　family-fear of　　ask+CAN-in case

　　I've got to hide from my relatives in case they ask me for things

7   Eylepere atyenge atnhe**mere-ketye**

　　leg　　me　　bite+CAN-in case

　　He might bite my leg

8   Tyerte-tyert-angkerrane elpathe**mere-ketye**

　　hide-hide-talking　　hear+CAN-in case

　　He is whispering because someone might hear him

9   Athe ampemere-ketye, waylpal-arenge pweleke ampe**mere-ketye**

　　grass burn+CAN-in case　　whitefella-'s　　cattle　　burn+CAN-in case

　　The grass might catch alight and burn the whitefella's cattle

9.3 'have been', 'used to', 'would': +yayne

If an action used to happen, or habitually happened, the ending used is +**yayne**. This ending is used when we would say in English 'has been', 'used to', 'would'.

10   Nterrenge aynanthe eyeyayne

　　seeds　　we　　grind+used to

　　We used to grind seeds

nterrenge eyayne

11   Alewatyerre nyarte aneyayne

　　goanna　　here　　sat+used to

　　A goanna has been here

12   Ngwetyanpe-ngwetyanpe weth-apenye rewenhe perrtyeyayne

　　morning-morning　　that-like　　himself　　tie+used to

　　Every morning he would tie his hair up like that

+**yayne** is also used if the action happened in the past but continued for some time, as in the next example:

Saturday aynanthe apenhe *football*-warle arewethe waylpel-eynenge

Saturday we went football-to see+PURP whitefella-lots

play-arreyayne

play-become-used to

On Saturday we went to the football to see the whitefellas playing

Here are the verb endings that show *tense*—that is, when an event happens—that you have learnt so far. The table below shows the tense endings for the verb **aynenke** 'eat'. Remember that +**yane** and +**rrane** go on intransitive verbs only.

Table 6   *Verb endings which mark tense*

tense	ending	verb form	English
past tense (habitual)	+**nye** / +**nhe** +**yayne**	**aynenye** **ayneyayne**	ate used to eat / would eat
present tense (incomplete)	+**nke** +**rrantye** / +**yane** / +**rrane**	**aynenke** **aynterantye**	eats is eating
future tense	+**ye** +**wethe**	**ayneye** **aynewethe**	will eat going to eat / should eat

9.4   'myself', 'yourself', 'one another', 'each other' [reflexive/reciprocal pronouns]

To say that someone is doing an action to themself, or a number of people are doing things to each other, a *reflexive* pronoun is used, just as we do in English ('myself', 'yourself', 'each other' etc.). In dialogue 9 you heard the reflexive pronoun **aylewenhanthe** 'ourselves' when the children said that they had been playing together (**elatneyayne**), and **ntewenhe** 'yourself' when the child was told to wash. Note how in Kaytetye a reflexive pronoun is used to say 'playing together' and 'washing yourself', whereas it is not used in the English phrase.

13   **Atyewenhe** ankwartetyele rntwenke

     myself   stone knife+with cut

     I cut myself with a knife

14   Alekele **rewenhe** atnhenhe

     dog+DOER itself   bit

     The dog bit itself

15   Rlwampel-amerne **atewenhanthe** angkenherre

     whitefella+DOER-PLURAL themselves   spoke

     The white men talked to one another

16   **Elwewenhanthe**   arlwenth+eynewethe

them two selves   marry+make+PURP

Let them marry each other

17   Artnwengele-therre   arwele   **elwewenhanthe**   eletnherrantye

child+DOER-two   stick   they two selves   throwing

The two children are throwing sticks at each other

Note

As we have seen, the 'doer' of a reflexive or reciprocal action must take the DOER marker (+**le** or +**nge**). The exception is where the doer in the sentence is representented only by a pronoun—as in examples 13 and 16 above.

Note that, like English, all reflexive sentences must have a reflexive pronoun in the sentence: you can't just add +**wenhe** onto the end of a noun. Below is the table of Kaytetye pronouns shown earlier, but this time with reflexive pronouns added.

Table 7   Kaytetye pronouns

	subject	object	possesive	reflexive
1st person singular	atye (doer) ayenge	atyenge	atyeyenge	atyewenhe myself
dual exclusive	aylanthe, aylenanthe	aylewanthe, aylekanthe	aylewantheyenge, aylekantheyenge	aylewenhanthe ourselves (2 people)
plural exclusive	aynanthe, aynenanthe	aynewanthe, aynekanthe	aynewantheyenge, aynekantheyenge	aynewenhanthe ourselves
2nd person singular	nte (doer) nge	ngkenge	ngkeyenge	ntewenhe yourself
dual	mpwelanthe	mpwewanthe	mpwewantheyenge	mpwewenhanthe yourselves (2 people)
plural	errwanthe	errwewanthe	errwewantheyenge	errwewenhanthe yourselves
3rd person singular	re	kwere	kwereyenge	rewenhe him/her/itself
dual	elwanthe	elwewanthe	elwewantheyenge	elwewenhanthe themselves (2 people)
plural	atanthe	atewanthe	atewantheyenge	atewenhanthe themselves

9.5 Ordering actions

In English we can show the ordering of actions by simply putting one action before the other, as in 'he eats and sleeps'. Another way is by using words such as 'while', 'during', or 'after'. In Kaytetye, word order won't tell you which action happens first. Instead you have to use endings which mean something like 'while', 'during', or 'after'.

'in order to', 'before something happens'

To say 'so that something else can happen' or that 'something happens first in order that something else can happen', the ending +**wethe-ketye** goes on the action that happens last, as you heard in dialogue 9. So in the phrase 'sits down so he can eat', +**wethe-ketye** would go on the verb 'eat'. This ending implies that the first action happens because the second action should happen; that is, that there is a connection between the two actions. These endings (combined) are glossed 'before'.

18   Re   alpereyne**wethe-ketye**   re   alhwengepe   etnpenke

        s/he   goes back+before   s/he   covers up   hole

        S/he covers the hole before s/he goes back

etnpenke

19   Artnangeynenye kwere, pakete kngwere aperneyne**wethe-ketye**

        moved   it   bucket another come+before

        They moved it before the other bucket came up/so that the other bucket could come up

20   Errkwene   ntewenhe ayne**wethe-ketye**

        wash+COMMAND yourself   eat+before

        Wash your hands before you eat!/so you can eat!

21   Nyarte anangeynene   nte ayenge ane**wetheketye**

        this   move+COMMAND you I   sit+before

        Move this thing out of the way so I can sit down

Something happens first

-**athathe** can be used to show that an action happens before the action with -**athathe** on it. This ending is also used on nouns (see section 11.5)

22   Weye nharte eytntene   nte pweweth-**athathe**(-ketye)

        meat   that   smell+COMMAND you cook+PURP-until(-in case)

        Smell that meat before you cook it

Another way to say that something comes first is to use the word **tangkwerle**.

 23   Mentye **tangkwerle** alele ampewethe

         leave   first   while   cook+PURP

         He lets them cook for a while first

24   Anewene **tangkwerle**

         sit+MUST   first

         You should let it sit for a while first

An action happens 'during' another event

To say that an action happens at the same time as something else is going on, or describe a time when another event happens, the ending -**ngareye** is used. It means 'when', 'at the time that…'. This ending goes on nouns.

 25   Atanthe apeyayteyayne tyanywenge-warle atherrkenye-**ngareye**

         they   come up+used to tobacco-to   green time-during

         They would come for tobacco during the green season

An action happens 'when', 'while' another action happens

To say that two actions happen at the same time as each other, the ending +**rewe** or -**rwenge** goes on the verb after the tense marking. It means 'while', 'when', 'at the same time as' the other action happens.

 26   Kwatheyayne-**rwenge** atanthe apenherre(pe)

         drink+used to-while   they   went(+FOCUS)

         He went while they were drinking

Notice in the following examples how the tense ending can change, but the +**rewe** ending still goes on after it.

 27   Re   apenherre-**rwenge** *store*-warle-rtame ayengepe apenke

         s/he   went-while   store-to-CONTRAST   I+FOCUS   go

         While he's gone, I'm going to the shop

28   Repe   apenke-**rewe**-rtame ayengepe *store*-warle-rtame apenke

         he+FOCUS   go+while-CONTRAST   I+FOCUS   store-to-CONTRAST   go

         When he goes, I'll go to the shop

Test your skill 9

Listen to dialogue 9 again. Write down the Kaytetye, and an English translation for it.

 Listen to these Kaytetye sentences on the CD and repeat them to yourself. Work out their meaning in English.

1   Atye kwere-ketye tyerte-akwerrantye.

2   Apenerne nge, ngkenge eletnhelayte+me-ketye!

3   Tyangkwerre apenerne nge ware ntheketyarte!

4   Elpere nge apene artweye-ketye.

5   Kartarte nge apene apmwe-ketye.

6   Aleke artnperraytenye nantewe-ketye.

7   Artweye+le antywe mpwarenhe arntwe+ketye.

8   Aleke+le atnheme+ketye errtywerne+le.

9   Lywekeyayne warepe, weyelke kwerarte pweyayne.

10   Atyewenhe arerrantye *glass*-le.

11   Atnkele-nhenge-therre+le alarrenhe elwewenhanthe.

12   Anthwerrke tangkwerle kwere arenhepe.

Dialogue 10   Wantertetye?

Vocabulary

Vocabulary

pwelkantye,		enewaylenge	echidna
amwelye	bearded dragon	kwathenke	drink
antere	fat	Ngalyerre	skin name
arlkarle	cold	pepe	book
atye	I	wenharte	that one just
aylake	we two		mentioned
artnpenke	run, walk around	etne	name

Further information

The word **wantertetye** means 'what sort of thing is that?' and is a good word to know for the Kaytetye learner. Another word with the same meaning is **wanterteyange**. It is made up of **wante+rteye+ange**.

10.1 Mistaken belief: something is not what it was thought to be

The ending **-athene** is added to words to show that something was not that thing, although you thought that it was; or that something was mistakenly done. In dialogue 10 the speaker thought the lizard was a dragon lizard but realised she was wrong and so said **pwelkantyew-athene**. The ending **-athene** is always preceded by the dative **+we**.

1   Re areynenge**w-athene** wenherre

    he euro+for-MISTAKE   shot

    He thought it was euro that he shot

2   Alepalele   kwenherre ahakeye**w-athene**

    unaware+DOER   swallowed   bush plum+for-MISTAKE

    (I) swallowed it, mistaking it for a bush plum

3   Arlenge-theye arelp-arenke   anatye**w-athene**

    long way-from   see while going bush potato+for-MISTAKE

    Looking from a distance I mistook them for bush potatoes

4   Ayenge etarrenhe errtyewarrerane**w-athene**

    I   thought   lying+for-MISTAKE

    I thought she was lying (but she wasn't)

Useful phrase

Tnhantew-athene re   nharte!

who+for-MISTAKE   s/he that

Who does he think he is!

10.2   'sort of', 'kind of'

The ending **-arrpanteye** or **-apartentye** can go on nouns to show that it's a bit like that thing, it's a pretend or fake one of those things. It can also be used to show that you don't really believe what is said. It is glossed 'sort of'.

5 *Doll-doll-***arrpanteye** artnwengele-therre mpwarerrantye

    dolls-sort of   child+DOER-two   making

    The two kids are making pretend dolls

6 Kakeytetherrele atyenge atnhenherre-rtame-**arrpanteye**

    scorpion+DOER   me   bit-CONTRAST-sort of

    It was something like a scorpion that bit me

7 Wante-rtetye nyartepe rlwen-**arrpanteye**?

    what-UNCERTAIN this+FOCUS bread-sort of

    Is this supposed to be bread?

10.3   'could', 'if you can/could'

To say that something can, might or could happen, or to say 'if something happens then…' you use the verb ending +**me** or +**mere**. Note how this verb ending is used in dialogue 10, where the women are dreaming about how they could eat or drink the pictures of things in the book. When +**me** or +**mere** is on a verb the doer can also have the ending **-apeke** or **-apekarre** to emphasise that the doer *might* do the action. (The ending +**arre** will be discussed further on in section 10.5.)

8 Apengele anatye kwerartepe apme**mere**-rtame, makwele

    go+S/A   potato   it+FOCUS   dig+CAN-CONTRAST   many

    If (we) go (we) can dig a lot of potatoes

9 Nyartepe nte enye malangke alepetye**mere**

    then+FOCUS you food nice   taste+CAN

    Then you can taste the nice fruit

10 Aynewethe, pwe**me**pe   kwere warele

    eat+PURP   cook+CAN+FOCUS it   fire+in

    To eat them you can cook them in the fire

11 Ahenange   ayenge ape**mere** errwanthel-arlenge?

    good+UNCERTAIN I   go+CAN   you lot+in-with

    Is it OK if I go with you lot?

Note

+**me** or +**mere** is the ending that **-ketye** follows when it occurs on a verb to mean 'something bad might happen' (section 9.4).

10.4   Sentences with more than one verb

Once you have mastered the use of simple sentences in Kaytetye, in particular those containing one verb, it is important to move on and learn how to make sentences that have more than one verb. For example, 'I *went* and *saw* the woman', or 'I *saw* the child *crying*.' Once you master this, you will find that the range of things you can say will increase greatly.

One very basic principle is this. When there are two verb actions in a sentence, it makes a difference whether they are being done by the same person ('I am sitting and talking') or by different people ('I am sitting and she is talking'): the grammar used is different in each case.

+ngele

In sentences where there are two or more actions (verbs) done by the one doer and the actions are closely connected, the two phrases can be joined by using the +**ngele** ending on one of the verbs. This translates in English as 'while doing' or 'and doing'. The ending is glossed s/A which stands for 'same actor' For example, look at the following two sentences:

 12   Ayenge anteyane
I am sitting

Ayenge angkerrane
I am talking

These can be joined by adding +**ngele** to one of the verbs, showing that the two actions happen at the same time:

 13   Ayenge ane**ngele** angkerrane

I	sit+s/A	talking

I am sitting talking

Listen and practise saying the following examples which are joined by using the +**ngele** ending.

 14   Ayenge artnpenherre

I	ran

I ran

Atye aherre   arenherre

I	kangaroo	saw

I saw a kangaroo

Atye artnpe**ngele** aherre   arenherre

I	run+s/A	kangaroo	saw

I saw a kangaroo while I was running

15   Atye aherre   arenherre

I	kangaroo	saw

I saw a kangaroo

Atye kwere aytnenyerre

I   it   speared

I speared it

Atye aherre   are**ngele** aytnenyerre

I   kangaroo   saw+s/a   speared

When I saw the roo I speared him

16   Atye arlkwerrantye

      I   waiting

      I am waiting

      Ayenge elyenge   entweyane

      I   shade+in   lying

      I am lying in the shade

      Ayenge elyenge arlkwe**ngele** entweyane

      I   shade+in   wait+s/a   lying

      I am lying in the shade, waiting

elyenge

+*ngewarle*

Take a case where the doers of the two sentences are different.

 17   Artweye apenherre

      The man went

      Atye artweye arenherre

      I saw a man

Notice how 'the man' is the actor in the first sentence but 'I' is the actor in the second. When two *different* people are doers in a combined sentence, they are joined with the ending +**ngewarle**. +**ngewarle** is glossed D/A which stands for 'different actor'.

 18   Artweye atye arenherre ape**ngewarle**

      man   I   saw   go+D/A

      I saw a man going

This ending was heard in dialogue 10 when the speaker said, 'I could eat that echidna that is walking on the rocks.'

If they were joined by +**ngele**, the meaning would be quite different:

 19   Artweye atye arenherre ape**ngele**

      man   I   see   go+s/a

      I saw a man *as I was going*

+**ngewarle** is also used in describing what someone says or thinks. Listen and practise saying the following examples which are joined with +**ngewarle**.

Beware
Sometimes **ngewarle** is pronounced **ngarle**.

20   Atye ngkenge elpathenke
     I   you   hear
     I hear you

     Nge angkerrane
     you talking
     You are talking

     Atye ngkenge elpathenke angke**ngewarle**
     I   you   hear   talk+D/A
     I hear you talking

21   Nte arenhe atyenge?
     you saw   me
     Did you see me?

     Ayenge artnpenherre
     I   ran
     I ran

     Arenhe nte atyenge artnpe**ngewarle**?
     saw   you me   run+D/A
     Did you see me run?

22   Re awely-awelye elpatheyerre
     he lightning   will hear
     He will hear the lightning

     Awely-awelyele weyerre
     lightning+DOER   will strike
     The lightning will strike

     Re elpatheyerre awely-awelyele weyerr**arle**/weng**arle**
     he will hear   lightning+DOER   hit+D/A
     He will hear the lightning striking

Note
When the ending **-warle** appears after the tense marker on the verb, it means the same as **-ngewarle**. This is what happens in example 22 above, the second time it is spoken.

23   Atye aweleyepe arenhe-rtame

I   uncle+FOCUS saw-EMPH

I saw my uncle

Aweleyelepe   arlweye alarrenherre

uncle+DOER+FOCUS father   hit

My uncle hit my father

Atye arenherre aweleyele   arlweye alarre**ngewarle**

I   saw   uncle+DOER father   hit+D/A

I saw my uncle hit my father

 24   *Tapem*-aylenye nte atyenge angke**ngewarle**

taped   you me   talk+D/A

You taped me talking

-penhe: 'after', 'from'

To say that something happens after something else, the ending **-penhe** goes on the verb stem preceded by a tense ending such as +**nke** or +**nhe**, or by +**nge**+.

 25   Weye nte ayneye(rre) atye artenke-**penhe**

meat   you eat+will   I   cut-after

You will eat the meat after I cut it up

26   Alemewane aynenye(rre)-**penhe**, alemepe   atyenge

sweet food   ate-after   stomach+FOCUS me

ahenelkeynenye(rre)

better+then+made

After eating sweet food I felt better

10.5   'that', 'since', 'whom', 'which' [relative clauses]

In English we often use 'that', 'who' or 'which' to add extra information which describes something about the main sentence. For example, 'the man *who hit me* might see you', 'I saw the man *that killed my dog*'. Notice how the part in italics provides extra information about the man. To say these kinds of sentences in Kaytetye we need to use a very different structure from the English one. Taking the first sentence above, you can see that it is made up of two parts.

 27   Artweyele ngkenge areme-ketye

man+DOER   you   can-in case

The man might see you

Artweyele atyenge alarrenhe

man+DOER   me   hit

The man hit me

To combine these, the ending +**arre** is added to the extra information. In dialogue 10 you heard the ending +**arre** on the word **arlkarle** 'cold'. If the person or thing which the extra information is about has an ending or is a doer, then the verb in this part of the sentence must take the same ending. Look at example 28 below. The extra information is 'who hit me', so +**arre** is on the word **atyenge** 'me'. The person who the extra information is about has the ending +**le**, so the verb too has this ending.

28 Artweyele atyeng**arre** alarrenhele ngkenge areme-ketye

man+DOER   me+that   hit+DOER   you   see+can-in case

The man who hit me might see you

Listen to how 'I saw the man who killed my dog' sounds in Kaytetye.

29 Artweye atye arenhe alek**arre** atyeyenge alarrenhe

man   I   saw   dog+that   my   killed

I saw the man who killed my dog

Listen to the following examples and pick out the two clauses.

30 Aynewanthe (re)   arntwenhe ng**arre**   apenhe

to us   s/he   told   you+that   went

He told us that you'd gone

Note
Some speakers use +**aye** instead of +**arre**, as in example 31 below.

---

31 Aynewanthe re   arntwenhe ng**aye**   apenhe

us   s/he   told   you+that   went

He told us that you'd gone

32 Aherre**we**   ayenge etnthwerrane artweyel**arre**   wenherre**we**

kangaroo+for   I   looking for   man+DOER+that   shot+for

I'm looking for the kangaroo that the man shot

Note
Some speakers, especially younger speakers, use the ending +**arle** instead of +**arre**. +**arle** is also the ending used by speakers of some other Arandic languages.

10.6   Kinship and skin names

Aboriginal social organisation is based on kinship, though the principles of this kinship system are very different from non-Aboriginal societies. Unlike the English system, the Kaytetye is an extended system which defines relationships between people who are not necessarily connected by birth links or by marriage, though Kaytetye people do distinguish 'close' and 'distant' kin.

Although it is beyond the scope of this book to deal with these concepts in depth, one aspect of the complex kinship system which is reflected in the Kaytetye language, and in the pronouns in particular, is the way people are divided into groups.

Kaytetye people belong to one of eight groups known as skin groups. This sort of name is refered to in Kaytetye as **ekwe**. Thus in addition to a personal name, the Kaytetye person acquires at birth not only an extended web of family relationships, but also a 'skin name' which partly defines their relationship to all other people within their language group and to others beyond.

Table 8   ***Kaytetye and other Central Australian skin names***

		Kaytetye	Eastern Anmatyerr	Alyawarr	Warumungu	Warlpiri
male	skin	Tyapalye Kapetye	Petyarr	Apetyarr	Jappaljarri	Japaljarri
female		Ngalyerre			Nappaljarri	Napaljarri
male	skin	Tyapeyarte Pengarte	Pengart		Jappangarti	Japangardi
female		Ngampeyarte			Nappangarti	Napangardi
male	skin	Tyakerre Kemarre	Kemarr	Akemarr	Jakkamarra	Jakamarra
female		Watyale			Nakkamarra	Nakamarra
male	skin	Mpetyakwerte Ampetyane	Ampetyan		Jamin	Jampijinpa
female		Tyamperlke			Nampin	Nampijinpa
male	skin	Tywekertaye Kngwarraye	Kngwarray	Kngwarrey	Jungarrayi	Jungarrayi
female		Ngapete			Namikili	Nungarrayi
male	skin	Tyaname Penangke	Penangk		Jappanangka	Japanangka
female		Ngamane			Nappanangka	Napanangka
male	skin	Tywelame Pwerle	Pwerl	Apwerl	Jupurla	Jupurrula
female		Ngamperle			Narurla	Napurrula
male	skin	Tyangkarle Thangale	Ngal		Jangala	Jangala
female		Ngangkarle/Ngale			Nangala	Nangala

These names provide a way of labelling and summarising a complex system of relationships and responsibilities between people, and between people and the land.

The name a person has depends on the skin names of each of their parents, but is not the same as that of either parent. To ask someone's skin name you use the question:

33 Wante-rtame ngepe   ekwepe?
what-EMPH   you+FOCUS skin+FOCUS
What's your skin name?

The eight skin names (or subsection names, as they are sometimes called) in Kaytetye and their corresponding names in the neighbouring languages are listed in table 8 above. Notice that in Kaytetye, Warlpiri and Warumungu there are female and male versions of each skin name. Listen to the Kaytetye skin names on the tape.

A person has the same skin name as, for example, their brothers and sisters, their father's father, and their father's brother's children. A person has a different skin from their mother, father, children and spouse.

Table 10 shows some of the relationships between the various groups or sections: who marries who, who is the father of who and so on. The gender-specific skin names are not included on the tables below. You can also see how this system divides into two *patrimoieties*.

Table 9   Patrimoieties

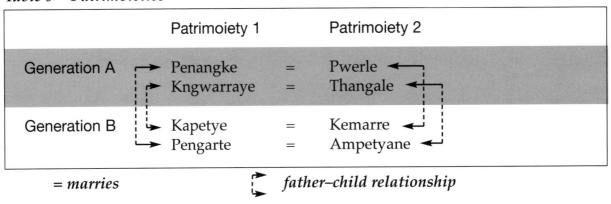

= *marries*   *father–child relationship*

From this diagram you can see, for example, that Ampetyane people marry Pengarte, Kapetye marry Kemarre, Penangke marry Pwerle and Kngwarraye marry Thangale. These marriage lines are shown by the = sign. The children of Kapetye men are Kngwarraye, the children of Pwerle men are Kemarre, the children of Thangale men Ampetyane, the children of Penangke men Pengarte and vice versa. The father–child relationships are shown by the arrow and you can see that the father and children are in the same patrimoiety, whereas the mother is in the opposite patrimoiety.

People belong to the same patrimoiety as their fathers, brothers and sisters, and their fathers' fathers, brothers' children etc. Patrimoieties tend to be important in land and Dreaming ownership, and in ceremony.

Another division you will notice is *generation moieties*:

Table 10   Generation moieties: **nywerrpe**

Generation moiety 1	Generation moiety 2
Thangale	Ampetyane
Kngwarraye	Kapetye
Pwerle	Kemarre
Penangke	Pengarte

A person belongs to the same generation moiety as their brothers, sisters, cousins, spouses, grandparents and grandchildren.

Generation moieties are important in ceremonies and in marriage patterns. It is preferred that a person marries into their own generation moiety. Whilst these moieties do not have names as they do in some other Aboriginal cultures, people in one generation moiety call people in the other **nywerrpe**. You are not supposed to marry someone who is **nywerrpe** to you—that is, of the other generation moiety.

Another division you will notice is *matrimoieties*. A person is in the same matrimoiety as their mother, mother's mother and their sister's children (or their own children if they are a woman).

Table 11   Matrimoieties

Matrimoiety 1	Matrimoiety 2
Penangke	Pwerle
Kngwarraye	Thangale
Kemarre	Kapetye
Ampetyane	Pengarte

How this influences the pronoun system

The Kaytetye pronoun system reflects the patrimoiety and generation moiety divisions. There is a set of dual and plural pronouns for people who are in the same patrimoiety and same generation (these plural pronouns have the +**angke** or +**angkerre** ending), another for people of the same patrimoiety but different generation (these pronouns are marked with the +**ake** or +**akerre** ending), and another for people of the opposite patrimoiety, so people in the opposite patrimoiety aren't distinguished for generation. These pronouns are marked with the +**anthe** or +**antherre** ending.

Table 3 (p. 71) shows only the set of pronouns for people in the opposite patrimoiety. These are also the pronouns to use if you are not sure of people's skins, and so are the *unmarked form*. The two other sets of kin-specific pronouns which show what sort of relations there are in a group of two or more people are shown in appendix 5 on pages 167–9.

10.7 Skin groups and social relationships

All this seems very complicated, but don't despair. It is beyond the scope of the beginning learner of these languages to master the system completely. Remember that Kaytetye children start learning these kin-specific words from very early on, whereas a person attempting to learn the pronouns first has to master the basics of the kin system itself.

Encoded in the kinship system are rules and conventions about marriage and behaviour towards particular kin. Some relationships between particular kin are characterised by easy-going interactions and joking, whilst between others, verbal communication and close contact are avoided altogether. This is sometimes called *avoidance* behaviour and the verb that describes this sort of behaviour in Kaytetye is **akerrentye**. The lack of appropriate social space between certain kin is sometimes referred to in English as 'no room'. So if someone says that there is 'no room' in a social situation the solution is not to clear a space, but rather to allow adequate social distance between relations who should not be near each other. This may mean that certain relations cannot, for example, travel in the same car together even though there appears to be plenty of 'room' in the back seat.

One of the strictest of these avoidance relationships is that between men and women who are in a mother-in-law/son-in-law relationship to each other. These relationships are Kemarre–Thangale, Kngwarraye–Pengarte, Ampetyane–Pwerle and Penangke–Kapetye. In table 9 you can see how the in-law relationship exists *within* one patrimoiety, but *across* adjacent generations. Ideally, in-laws should not sit together or travel close together and they should exchange goods and messages through a third person.

There are even special words in Kaytetye used by women to talk about their sons-in-law, and by men to talk about their mothers-in-law. For example, some women use the word **arrempelarreyern-alpenke** for 'come' when they are talking about their sons-in-law, and the word **apenkerne** for 'come' when they are talking about anyone else. They would also use **entywerre** instead of **arntwe** for 'water'. There are many other special verbs and other words in this language, although they are not used as much as they used to be. An example of a sentence in this kind of language is as follows:

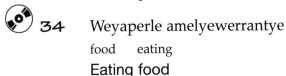 34   Weyaperle amelyewerrantye

        food   eating

        Eating food

In so-called 'normal' language this sentence would be:

    35   Enye aynterantye

        food   eating

        Eating food

In Kaytetye there are many words to describe actual relations: words for mother, father, uncle, cousin etc. Remember that these do not always work the same way as such family words do in English: for example, in English your father's brother's children are called cousins, whereas in Kaytetye they are called brothers and sisters. There are also generally four kinds of grandparent (and grandchild) recognised: mother's mothers, mother's fathers, father's fathers and father's mothers. The gender of these four kinds of grandparents is not distinguished, so the word for father's father can also apply to father's father's sister. The terms for these four grandparents are also 'two-way', so grandparents of a particular type and their grandchildren call each other by the same kin term. This is unlike English, where the terms 'grandparent' and 'grandchild' are used. These family words are also used to describe the relationship between people and country and Dreamings.

We have touched briefly on a few sets of ideas that are interwoven and connected in ways that are a bit difficult to visualise: the skin names, words used to describe certain kin (such as mother, father, cousin etc.), and the idea of kin being split into groups or moieties showing patrimoiety and generation level.

The diagram below is a fragment of a family tree drawn from the perspective of a **Watyale** (Kemarre woman). Shown here are the skin names of some of the close relations of Watyale, and the kin terms, or Kaytetye words for 'father', 'mother' etc., that *she* would call these respective relations.

Table 12   Part of the family tree of a Watyale woman showing the skin names and kin terms she would use for some of her relations

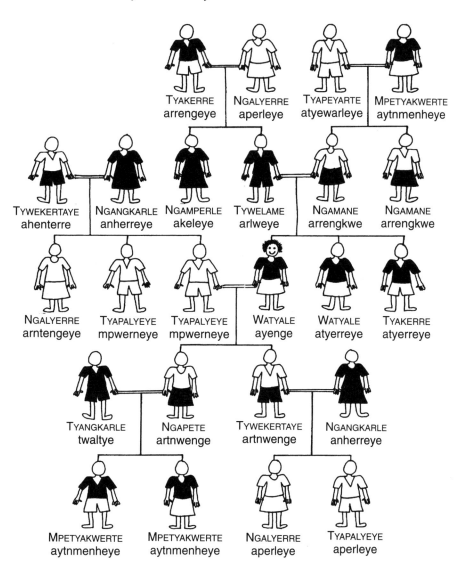

To represent the idea of division into groups, the relations who belong to the opposite generation moiety or are **nywerrpe** to Watyale have black shorts or skirts, and those who are in the same generation moiety have white. You can see clearly from this that people in the generation level immediately before and immediately after Watyale are **nywerrpe** to her, whereas those two levels away belong to the same generation moiety as her—for example her grandparents and grandchildren. Those with black shirts belong to the same patrimoiety as Watyale and those with white shirts belong to the other. It must be emphasised that this diagram represents only a small part of the potential close family of a Watyale; you have to imagine this network extending out in all directions, in fact in ways that are difficult to show in two dimensions.

Test your skill 10

Listen to dialogue 10 again. Write down the Kaytetye, and an English translation for it.

Fill in the following family tree from the perspective of a different skin, naming both the kin and skin names of each person with respect to yourself, or to an Ampetyane man or woman.

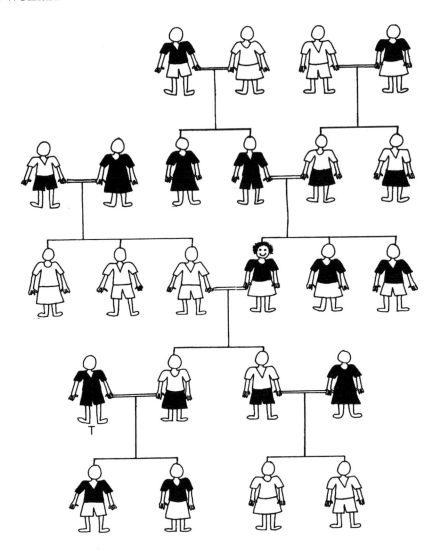

Listen to these Kaytetye sentences on the CD and repeat them to yourself. Work out their meaning in English.

1 Nt+apek+arre aherre alarre+mere, akelye nte atyenge alperneyne+wethe weye?

2 Repe apenherre aherre+w-athene wenhe.

3 Mentye re angke+ngele ape+wene.

4 Re angke+ngele etnthwerrane.

5 Atye artnpe+ngele arenhe aherre.

6 Atye aherre are+ngele aytnenye.

7 Ayenge angke+ngele anteyane.

8 Arlkwe+ngele elye+nge anteyane(re).

9 Arrknge kwathenhe-penhe weye akely-apeke re aynenyerre.

10 Kwelharre nte ayneye aty+arre aytne+nge-penhe.

11 Atye arenherre atherrke aynterantye+nge-warle elentye+le.

12 Artweye atye arenke ape+nge-warle.

13 Atye ngkenge elpathenke angke+nge-warle.

14 Aherr+arre ampwarrenhe-warle nge apene!

15 Aherre+we ayenge etnthwerrane artweye+l-arre wenhe+we.

Dialogue 11   Wante nte mpwarerrantye?

Vocabulary

akaltyarrenke	learn	artnwenge	child
akaltyeynenke	teach	elye	shade, bough shed
alperre	leaf	mpwarenke	make
arrenke	put	arrkantel-arknge	for fun

Further information

Elye not only refers to shade structures that people make, but also to naturally occurring shade and shadows, anywhere out of the sun's direct rays.

11.1 'with', 'accompanied by', 'together'

The ending **-arlenge** has a range of meanings but it can be used to show that two elements in a sentence are equally involved in the action of the event, or that the two things in general play the same role. In general, two things connected by **-arlenge** must be of the same type, for example, people together, or inanimate objects together. It translates as 'with', 'together', 'along with' , 'in the company of' and sometimes as 'in' or 'inside'. This ending goes on nouns, and is always preceded by the +**le**/+**nge** ending.

1   Anyene   nte   atnwenthe+**l-arlenge**   pwewethe
       onion   you   meat+in-with   cook+PURP
       You cook onions with meat

2   Angerrentye   eyterrtye+**l-arlenge**   anteyane
       spirit   body+in-with   sitting
       The spirit is in the body

3   Atyerreyaye!   Atyenge+**l-arlenge**   anewethe
       younger sibling+hey   me+in-with   sit+PURP
       Younger brother, stay with me

4   Atyenge+**l-arlenge**   angkenke   re
       me+in-with   talking   s/he
       He's talking with me

5   Mpwerneyaye!   Ngepe   atyenge+**l-arlenge**   apenerne!
       brother-in-law+EMPH   you+FOCUS   me+in-with   come+COMMAND+this way
       Brother-in-law, come with me!

6   Re   atyenge   alarrenhe   kwere+**l-arlenge**
       s/he   me   hit   her/him+in-with
       S/he hit me because of him/her

~~~~~~

Note

+**l-arlenge** is actually made up of +**le** ('on', 'at') plus -**arlenge**. This means that if the word it attaches to is a short word, the form of this ending changes to +**ng-arlenge** (+**nge** plus -**arlenge**). For example:

> arntwe**ng-arlenge**
>
> water+in-with
>
> with water

> erlkwe**ng-arlenge**
>
> old man+in-with
>
> with the old man

Sometimes +**l-arlenge** can have other meanings than 'with', such as **arrkantel-arlenge** 'for fun', as you heard in dialogue 11 and **marntel-arlenge** 'by bus'.

 7   Ayenge apenhe-ngerne marnte**l-arlenge**

> I   came-this way   bus+in-with
>
> I came on the bus

Note

Marnte 'bus' can be either +**le** or +**l-arlenge** to mean 'by bus'.

One of the important considerations in this type of Kaytetye sentence where there are two people, or animals, etc. doing something together is who is the controller or initiator of the action. This is often the more senior person.

There is a difference between 'two people just going along together' and one or other of the individuals 'taking the other along' and this difference in meaning determines which ending should be used. Earlier we looked at the ending -**akake,** which can also mean 'with'. Consider the following example:

 8   Ayenge alek-**akake** apenherre

> I   dog-having   went
>
> I went with the dog

but the following sentence does not sound right…

9 ✗ Ayenge aleke**l-arlenge** apenherre

> I   dog+in-with   went
>
> I went with the dog (together)

11.2 'so that…'

In chapter 10 you learnt how to make complex sentences by doing things such as joining clauses together in one sentence (using more than one verb). Another kind of complex sentence is involved if you want to say 'so that somebody or something can do something'. Here you use the endings **-aytenge** or **-angkarrenye** on the noun (which is often a pronoun) instead of on the verb. You heard this in dialogue 11 on the pronoun **atye** when the speaker said '…so that I can make the bough shed'. Listen to the following examples which also use **-aytenge**:

10 Arntwe arrer-apenye atnarrewethe alekel-**aytenge** kwatherrantye+wethe
water   close-like   put+PURP   dog+DOER-so that drinking+PURP

Put the water closer so that the dog can drink it

11 *Cool drink* kwere   nte etnyene   (nte) **raytenge**/**rangkarrenye**
soft drink him/her you give+COMMAND (you) s/he+so that

kwathewethe
drink+PURP

Pass her the soft drink so she can have a drink

~~~~~~

Note
-aytenge can also be pronounced **-aytenye**. Beware, however, as this can also occur on nouns that express qualities, such as 'bad' or 'good', and in that case **-aytenye** means 'more of that quality'.

Ahen-aytenye nharte atyenge etnyene   nte!
good+INTENSIFIER that   me   give+COMMAND you
Give me that better one!

~~~~~~

11.3 Doing something for/on behalf of somebody else

To say that you are doing something for somebody else, or on their behalf, such as 'getting something for somebody else', 'taking something for somebody else' you use the noun **katye** before the verb. You heard this in dialogue 11, and earlier, in dialogue 5, when one speaker asked the other to get petrol for him.

12 Tyanywenge Ngampwerlewe **katye**   eylewethawe!
tobacco   Ngampwerle+for on behalf get+PURP+hey
Hey get some tobacco for Ngampwerle!

13 Elkwemen-eynengewe **katye**   alpereyneyayne atnwenthe aynanthe
old women-lots+for   on behalf bring back+used to meat   we
We would bring back some meat for the old women

11.4 'as far as', 'up to'

To say 'as far as' or 'up to' you use the ending +**w-artetye**, which is really made up of +**we** plus -**artetye**. This ending marks where an action or event ends. -**artetye** is also used on times and dates to mean, for example, 'until 5.00 p.m.'.

14 Nthe**wartety**arte ayenge apenherre

    that+as far as+DEM   I   went

    I went as far as that

15 Elpaye**w-artetye** ayenge apenherre, areynengewe

    creek+for-as far as   I   went   euro+for

    I went as far as the creek, looking for euros

16 Ntheke**w-artetye** nge apenke?

    where+for-as far as you going

    How far are you going?

17 Tye**w-artetye** atye aylenke

    this+for-as far as I   sing

    This is as far as I can sing [the dreaming song]

18 Kngwer-amerne apeyayne Aileron-**wartetye**

    another-PLURAL   go+used to Aileron-for-as far as

    Others used to go as far as Aileron

19 *Monday*-theye *Friday*-**wartetye**

    Monday-from   Friday+for-as far as

    From Monday to Friday

11.5 'until', 'before'

To say 'until' in the sense of 'until something gets to a certain stage', you use the ending -**athathe**. It can go on both nouns and verbs. On nouns it is preceded by the endings +**we** or -**warle**. For example, *school*-**wathathe** means 'before/until school (starts)'. On verbs -**athathe** is preceded by the purposive ending +**wethe**, as you saw in section 9.5.

20 Ware arrpeyayne   errtywele kwere**w-athathe** akarreyneyayne

    fire   make a fire+used to kindling   it+for-until   gather+used to

    We would make a fire by gathering all the kindling until it was big enough

21 Atantherre wampere etntye   apereyneyayne arlpalhe**w-athathe**

    they   possum   hair/fur take+used to   string+for-until

    They would take the possum fur before making it into string

22 Alele aylanthe anteyane *Tuesday*-**wathathe**

    soon   we   sitting   Tuesday+for-until

    We are staying until Tuesday

23	Weye nharte eytntene	nte pweweth-**athathe**
	meat that smell+COMMAND	you cook+PURP-until

Smell that meat before you cook it

11.6 Word building

Kaytetye has many ways of making new words from others. Here are some examples of how to expand your Kaytetye vocabulary by learning these tricks.

Loan words

Like any language, Kaytetye borrows words. In recent times many new words have been borrowed from English—often with a rather different meaning from the English meaning, and often pronounced in a distinctly Kaytetye way. In fact, they may sound quite different from the way an English speaker would say them. Kaytetye people who are literate in their own language may also decide to spell these words in a Kaytetye way. The following are examples:

24
mwetekaye	car, motor vehicle	*(from English 'motorcar')*
tyampete	billycan	*(from English 'jam pot')*
terethe	dress	*(from English 'dress')*
warrke	work	*(from English 'work')*

Making intransitive verbs

When +**arre**+ is added to a noun, the resulting verb generally means 'become (more) of that thing, quality or state'. +**arre**+ generally means 'become', 'get'. Tense endings are then added as they would be for any other verb.

Beware
Do not confuse this with the relative clause marker +**arre**, which was discussed in section 10.5.

In dialogue 11 when Ampetyane asked 'what are they learning?' you heard her use the word **akaltye** 'knowledgeable' plus +**arre**+, making it into a verb meaning '(to) learn'. Here are some other examples:

25
ahene	good	ahenarrenke	get better

26
pantye	blanket	pantyarrenke	lay down

27
kwetnaye	tired	kwetnayarrenke	get tired

28
errpatye	bad	errpatyarrenke	spoil

29
warrke	work	warrkarrenke	work

~~~~~~

Note

akaltye plus the verb **etnyenke** 'give' also combine to mean 'teach', as you heard earlier on.

~~~~~~

Making transitive verbs

In a similar way **+ayle+** or **+eyne+** can be added to a noun and the resulting verb has the meaning of 'make (more) of that thing, quality or state'. In dialogue 11 you heard the word **akaltye** 'knowledgeable' plus +**eyne**, making it into a transitive verb meaning 'teach'.

30	ahene	good	aheneynenke	make better
31	akaltye	knowing, knowledgeable	akaltyeynenke	teach
32	kwetnaye	tired	kwetnayeynenke	make tired
33	aynterrke	dry	aynterrkeynenke	make dry
34	makwele	lots	makwerlaylenke	make lots, pile up

~~~~~~

Note

The above examples can take +**ayle** or +**eyne**; however, for English words borrowed into Kaytetye +**ayle** is always used.

~~~~~~

Kaytetye transitive verbs can also be made from English verbs by adding +**ayle** 'make', which is preceded by +**em**.

35	*pay*-emaylenke	buy, pay
36	*drive*-emaylenke	drive
37	*clean*-emaylenke	clean the place up

~~~~~~

Further information

In Pidgin English transitive verbs include the marker +**em**, which is based on hearing the 'him' or 'them' after an English transitive verb, such as 'pay them', 'catch him'. Kaytetye, and many other Aboriginal languages, continue the pattern of borrowing +**em** when using an English transitive verb.

~~~~~~

When nouns are made into verbs in this way the endings +**lke** and -**rtame** can occur before the +**eyne**/+**ayle**/+**arre** part of the verb. Listen to the following verb forms.

38   Ayenge erlkwe**lk**-arrenhe
          I   old man+now-became
     I got older

39   Alwengke+**lke-rtame**-nte-eynenyerre?
          forget+now-EMPH-you-made
     Did you forget it?

40   Kwerepenhepe aherrkepe atwerrpe**lk**-arrenherre
          after that+FOCUS   sun+FOCUS   afternoon+now-became
     Then the sun got low on him

41   Pwele-pwele(-penhe)pe kngwere**l-ayethe**lk-arrenke angkety-akakelke
          tadpole(-from)+FOCUS   other+on-facing+then-becomes   feet-having+then
     He changes from a tadpole, then he gets feet

Note
Pronouns can also occur before the +**eyne**/+**ayle**/+**arre** part of the verb, and after the endings +**lke** and +**rtame**, as you heard in example 39 above.

Test your skill 11
Listen to dialogue 11 again. Write down the Kaytetye, and an English translation for it.

Listen to these Kaytetye sentences on the CD and repeat them to yourself. Work out their meaning in English.

1   Nthakenh-arreyayne nge kwenyele?

2   Ayenge alther+arrenke apmere atyeyenge+we.

3   Methethe+l-arlenge artntepe ethwenke.

4   Re apenherre Pmangker-areny-eynengel-arlenge.

5   Ngkenge+l-arlenge ayenge apenk-apertame.

6   Erlkwe anteyane amarle+l-arlenge.

7   Amarle aperrane erlkwe+ng-arlenge.

8   Erlkwety-erlkwe+we katye alpereyneyayne apmere-warle weye.

9   Re alpereyne+weth-athathepe arreyerre awenyerre+l-angene-rtame, kwerrke-warle arreyerre.

10   Ayenge apenke warrk+arre+wethe.

11   Wante-penhe nge akerleyt+arrerane?

12   Alkaperte ape atye arntwerantye atnawerr+eyne+wethe atewenhanthe+le-therre.

13   Renh+arre alemewane aynenye-penhe, alemepe atyenge ahenelk+eynenye.

Dialogue 12 Wantewarte artnwenge nhartepe akerrane?

Vocabulary

akenke	cry	ekwele	sulky
akerleyte	quiet	rewenhe elpatherrantye	feel
alantye	anyway, regardless	ngwenge	tomorrow
apeyaytenke	come	rlengke	today
arntetye	sick		

Further information

In Kaytetye the word **artnwenge** 'child' is a common way to address both daughters and sons, and so in this situation it is best translated as 'daughter' or 'son'.

12.1 'feel'

Using *aleme*

One way to say 'feel' is by using the word **aleme** 'stomach'. You have already heard this in dialogue 7: **aleme ayenge angayele**, meaning 'I'm hungry'.

 1   **Aleme** ayenge arntetye

       stomach I   sick

       I feel sick

    2   **Aleme** ayenge ahenelk-arrenhe

       stomach I   good+now-became

       I got better then

Further information

Whereas in English we regard the heart as the seat of emotions, in Kaytetye it is the stomach. There are many idioms to describe feelings in Kaytetye made up from **aleme**, such as **aleme angkerrane**, 'jealous', which literally means 'stomach talks', and **alemele arenke** 'to have a premonition', which literally means 'stomach sees'.

Using a reflexive pronoun

In dialogue 12 you heard another way to say 'feel', when the speaker asked if the child felt sick. Here she used the verb **elpatherrantye** 'hear' and a reflexive pronoun **atyewenhe** meaning 'herself'. This doesn't mean 'hear myself', 'yourself' etc., it means 'feel' and can be used for feeling sad, sick, angry and so on.

 3   **Atyewenhe elpatherrantye** arntetye

       myself   hearing   sick

       I feel sick

12.2   How an action is done—in what manner

These are words used to show the speed at which an action happened, the degree of force used to perform the action and to provide other information about how the action happened, such as whether or not the action was completed successfully. These words are a bit like English *adverbs*.

 4

etak-etake, mwantye	carefully
kartarte	slowly
alhewere	anyway, without restrictions
alantye	do anyway, heedless
elpere, awere, apapenye	quickly
alele, apertangkwerle	in a minute
elapenye	for a while, slowly, always
artewentye	forcefully, extremely, strong
alepale	unaware, in ignorance
aytnarne	in vain, unable

5   Atnwenthele areme-ketye **etak-etake nge** kengarrenhe
    meat+DOER   see+in case   carefully   you sneaked up
    You sneaked up *carefully* so the animal didn't see

6   **Apapenye** atanthe kwere ekngethele-wenke
    quickly   they   him   decorate
    They decorate him as *quickly* as possible

7   Elyengelke **aytnarne** aweparerane
    Shade+in+now   in vain   waiting
    He is waiting in the shade *in vain*

8   Aterarrenge-wanenye nge **alhewere**
    scared+become-not   you   confident
    You can't be scared, you've got to be *confident*

Further information
'twice' or 'three times' is said by putting the ending **-rwenge** on a number word.

 9

   therre-**rwenge** atye alarrenhe
   two-times   I   hit
   I hit it twice

10   Errkwentye-**rwenge** re ahelaytnenye
    three-times   he called out
    He called out three times

In lesson 7 you learnt to use the noun ending **-apenye** to say that something is similar to something else. This ending can also be used on some manner words, like the ones above, to mean something like the English 'er' in words like 'slow*er*', 'quick*er*'

11 Kartart-**apenye** nge aweparene

    slowly-like   you wait+COMMAND

    Go slower, take it easy

12.3 'can't', 'unable', 'tried to'

To say that you wanted to do something but weren't able to, or that you nearly achieved something, or missed out on something, then the ending +**weth-anenhe** goes on the verb. You heard this towards the end of dialogue 12.

12 Akwerteytengele atewanthe ayne**weth-anenhe**

    rainbow snake+DOER   them   eat+PURP-nearly

    The rainbow snake nearly ate them

13 Atye ayne**weth-anenhe** alekele nharte eylelaytenye

    I   eat+PURP-nearly   dog+DOER that   got&go away

    I didn't get to eat it, as the dog ran off with it

14 Ayenge atnwenthewe ape**weth-anenhe**

    I   meat+for   go+PURP-nearly

    I wanted to go for meat but couldn't

12.4 Location and direction

Location of people and events within the geographical landscape is of utmost importance to the Kaytetye, who learn from early childhood how to place themselves within space and within their country. In fact some childhood games rely on a very sound knowledge of direction. The Kaytetye words used to describe the compass directions—north, south, east, and west—may be used to talk about movement and direction over long distances or to talk about movements made on a small scale, for example telling someone how to draw a shape on paper or which direction to move a swag (whereas in English the words 'left' and 'right' are usually used).

The compass direction words are as follows:

15

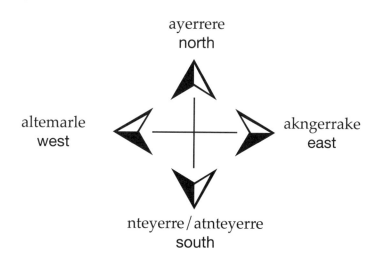

ayerrere
north

altemarle
west

akngerrake
east

nteyerre / atnteyerre
south

~~~~~~

Further information

The words for north-east, south-west etc. are made by using the ending **-apenye**, so 'north-east' or 'north-west' is:

   ayerrer-**apenye**

and 'north-west' or 'south-west' is:

   altemarl-**apenye**

~~~~~~

Here are some useful words that describe location or movement of people, objects or places with respect to a speaker.

 16

akanpere	past, beyond
anthenayne	on the other side
mwernenye	on this side, close
aylke	head side
mpwarle	foot side
ngkwethe	the side
mwernarte	facing this way, facing something
eyntwemele	facing away from
aywerrpe	across, crossways
anwengere	outside
kwene	inside
arrwekele	in front
atntengetheye	behind
elkwerre	middle, in between
rlweynteme	opposite, wrong way

'towards', 'in the direction of': -atheke

Another ending that shows that the action or the motion is aimed towards a place, a person or a thing is **-atheke**. It is commonly used in describing directions.

17 Alpenherre akngerrak-**atheke**, apmwe ahenenye-therre

   went   east-towards   snake   woma python-two

   The two snakes travelled towards the east

18 Kwere-penhe aynanthe apenherre akngerrak-**atheke**

   it-after   we   went   east-towards

   After that we went eastwards

19 Merlentyarl-**atheke** nthewartetyarte

   Merlentye+to-towards   there+far as+DEM

   They went as far as there, to Merlentye

20 Nharte kwere apmeyerre-apertame kwenel-**atheke**

   then   it   dig+will-again   under+at-towards

   Then you dig down further

21 Artepel-arerrantye rlweyntem-atheke anteyane
    back+at-looking   other way-towards   sitting
    He has his back to me, facing the other way

22 Atyengarl-**atheke** mwernart-arrenhe
    me+to-towards   this way-became
    It is facing this way, towards me

23 Akngerrak-**atheke** arenhe, arltemarl-**atheke** arenhe 'Apeyakele'
    east-towards   saw   west-towards   saw   nothing
    (He) looked to the east and he looked to the west, (and thought) 'All right, there is nothing there'

24 *Barrow Creek*-theye mwernart-aperte, atnteyerre-**atheke**
    Barrow Creek-from   this way-just   south-towards
    From Barrow Creek (it is) this way, southwards

12.5 Position and stance

There are a number of endings which can be put on nouns to describe the type of position the nouns are in. This is a bit similar to English phrases such as 'backwards', 'sideways' 'face up' etc. A few of these will be discussed below.

'facing'

The ending +**l-ayethe** is used to describe a position or stance, particularly with body parts, where the body part with the +**l-ayethe** ending is the part touching the surface. It is also sometimes used on other nouns where the meaning is less predictable.

25 aleme**l-ayethe**

    stomach+on-facing
    face down

26 artepe**l-ayethe**

    back+on-facing
    face up

27 kngwere**l-ayethe**

    other+on-facing
    other way

28 Rlwene   aynanthe akwerre**l-ayeth**-apertame etnyeyayne
    vegetable food we   coolamon+on-facing-again   give+used to
    We would give them bush tucker served in the coolamon

Further information

The ending **-angene** means 'side', and is preceded by the **+le** (*locative*) ending. For example, **awenyerr+l-angene** 'on one side'. The word for 'early evening' is made up from this ending, joined onto the word for 'afternoon', **atwerrpe+l-angene**.

12.6   Complex verbs

So far we have only talked about the situation where you add one ending to the verb stem. Kaytetye verbs are often very complex with many endings stacked on after the verb stem. Take the following verb for example:

 29   kwathe+rrapereynterantye+wethe+pe

       drink+while going along+PURP+FOCUS

       should be drinking while going along

Sometimes it is useful to think of the verb as having slots into which various bits or endings can fit. Fortunately for the learner not all the slots need to be filled, though it is a minimum requirement that the verb contain its stem and one other ending.

Some of the most common endings heard on Kaytetye verbs tell you what sort of motion is associated with the verb. For example, if the person came and did the verb, went and did the verb, did the verb and then went, did the verb once as they went along, etc. While there are too many of these endings to cover in this learner's guide, below are some of the more common ones; all of them occur after the verb stem and before the tense ending.

'when it comes'

To say that a person or thing came up and then the action happens to that person or thing, the ending **+y-ayte+** is put on the verb stem. The thing or person that comes up is not the same person or thing doing the main action:

 30   Weye atyenge etnye**y-ayt**enye artweyele

       meat   me   gave-it came   man+DOER

       The man gave me some meat when I came up

    31   Atye kwere arwelele alarre**y-ayt**enyerre

       I   it   stick+with hit-it comes

       I hit it with a stick when it came to me

~~~~~~

Note

When +**y-ayte**+ occurs on motion verbs it doesn't have this meaning. In fact, the meaning of the motion verb is nearly the same whether it has +**y-ayte**+ or not.

32   Ayenge alpe**y-ayt**enye apmere-warle

   I   returned   camp-to

   I came back to the camp

33   Ayenge alpenhe apmere-warle

   I   returned   camp-to

   I returned to the camp

You heard **apeyaytenke** in dialogue 12, where it meant 'come'.

~~~~~~

There are also some verbs that have +**yayte**+ as part of their stem. These verbs always have the +**yayte**+ on them—it's not an ending so you can't leave it out, which is why they don't have a hyphen:

34   atnthe**yayt**enke   climb, ascend
     atne**yayt**enke   get up

'go back and do'

In Kaytetye it is common to say 'go back and do such and such' by putting +**y-alpe**+ before the tense ending.

35   *dinner* aynanthe ayne**y-alpe**wethe

   dinner   we   eat-go back &+PURP

   Let's go back to eat lunch

36   Apmere-warle atanthe enwe**y-alp**enherre

   camp-to   they   lay-go back &

   They went back and camped

'go and do'

To say 'go and do such and such' the ending +**y-ene**+ is added to the verb stem:

37   Elyenge re   ane**y-ene**nke

   shade+in s/he sit-go &

   S/he goes and sits in the shade

38   Arntetye atye are**y-ene**wethe

   sick   I   sit-go &+PURP

   I'm going to visit the sick person

'do and go'

To say 'do something and go' the ending +**l-ayte**+ is put on the verb stem if the verb is transitive—for example, **arel-ayt**enke 'have a look and go'. A further example is:

 39   Arekenye-warle re   arre**l-ayt**enke apmere-warle re   alpereynenke

          shovel-to   s/he puts-&go   camp-to   s/he takes

          He puts it in the shovel and takes it back to camp

If the verb is intransitive (so the action is not being done *to* someone or something) the ending +**rr-ayte**+ is used:

 40   Elper-aperte aherre   artnpe**rr-ayt**emere-ketye!

          quickly-just   kangaroo   run-&go+can-in case

          Quickly, before the kangaroo runs away!

'do while going'

To say 'do something while going' the ending +**rr-ape**+ is put on the intransitive verb, while the ending +**rr-apereyne**+ is used if the verb is transitive, for example:

 41   Aynanthe are**rr-apereyn**terantyewethe alewatyerrewe

          we   look-while going+PURP   goanna+for

          We'll go looking for goanna

      42   Artweyele are**rr-apereyn**terantyengele arlelke   aperranengele

          man+DOER   look-while going+S/A   hunting   goes+S/A

          The man goes along looking as he goes hunting

'do and return'

To say 'do something and go back' the ending +**l-alpe**+ is put on the verb stem if the verb is transitive. For example:

 43   Pwelekele arntwe kwathe**l-alp**enke

          cattle+DOER   water   drink-&return

          The cattle had a drink of water and went back

Note

Sometimes the ending +**y-alpe**+ and +**rr-alpe**+ can be used with this meaning:

      enthwe**y-alp**enke   look around before going back

 44   Eylkwennge antye**y-alp**enke alhwenge-warl-atheke

          mouse   jump-&return   hole-to-towards

          The mouse jumps as he goes back towards his hole

'coming this way doing'

If an action is being done at the same time as the person doing the action is coming towards the speaker, then +**yern-alpe**+ is added to the verb stem. It is often translated as 'came along doing such and such'.

 45 eyle**yern-alp**enhe came along and got (them)

ater-etnye**yern-alp**enhe came along and gave (them) a fright

'do after getting up'

You can also use +**yern-ayte**+ to show that an action happens after getting up. For example:

 46 Ngwetyanpe-ngwetyanpe perrtye**yern-ayte**nye rewenhe

morning-morning tie up-after getting up+PAST himself

Every morning after getting up, he would tie (his hair) up

'happens on the way'

If an action happens as the person is going along, or moving in some way, then +**lp**- is added to the verb stem and then the part before the +**lp**- is repeated. Verbs with this ending can also have other meanings such as that the action is starting to happen, happening bit by bit or happening repeatedly. Look at these forms:

 47
arenke	see	arelp-arenke	sees on the way
atnywenke	enter	atnywelp-atnywenke	go in on the way
kwathenke	drink	kwathelp-athenke	sip
alarrenke	hit	alarrelp-arrenke	hits on the way/ pat something

48 Aherre nharte atye alarre**lp-arr**enke

kangaroo that I hit-on the way

I hit the kangaroo while I was driving

49 Pweleke artnperr-aytenyerre makwele-warle (re) atnywe**lp-atnywe**nye

cattle ran-&go many-to (s/he) entered-on the way

The bullock ran away and went into the herd

Notice that it is always only the vowel, consonant sound and vowel closest to the +**lp**- which is reduplicated.

'doing all the way around', 'all the way along'

If an action is being done continuously as the person is going along, or the action extends over an entire space, then +**l**- is added to the verb stem and then the part before the +**l**- is repeated with +**l-arre**+ attached to the end, before the tense ending. Consider the following forms:

50	eylenke	get	eylel-**eylel-arre**nke	gets (them) all the way

50	eylenke	get	eylel-**eylel-arre**nke	gets (them) all the way
	alarrenke	hit	alarrel-**arrel-arre**nke	hits (them) all the way
	arenke	see	arel-**arel-arre**nke	watches (them) all the way

51 Wey-apeke   alarrel-**arrel-arre**rantye (re)
animal-perhaps   hitting-all the way   (it)
S/he's killing meat while going along

If the verb is intransitive, then +**rr-** is added to the verb stem and then the part before the +**rr-** is repeated with +**rr-etnye**+ attached to the end, before the tense ending:

52	antyenke	jumps
	antye**rr-antyerr-etnye**rrane	jumping while moving
	enwenke	lie
	entwe**r-entwer-etnye**rrane	lying all around

53 Aynanthe awenyerrame atnte**r-atnter-etnye**rrane
we   one by one   standing-all the way
We stand around one by one

Notice that some of these verbs don't involve movement, instead they show that something is distributed around.

Note
+**rr-...rr-etnye**+ becomes +**r-...r-etnye**+ if the verb has any of the sounds in columns 3–5 on page 10 before the verb ending.

Plural marking on the verb

You learnt in section 2.5 that one way to show that there is more than one person is to use the endings **-therre**, **-amerne**, or **-eynenge** on the noun. If the person or thing doing the action is more than two, that is, there is a group of them, then another way to show this is to reduplicate part of the verb, the action that they are doing. In this case the first two-syllable section of the verb stem is reduplicated.

54 Kngwere **alweng-alweng**ayey-ayteyayne weyewe
others   ask-ask-it came+used to   meat+for
Others would ask him for meat after he got there

55 **Lweme-lwem**-aneyerre atanthepe akwelyelke elpatheyerre
come out-come out-sit+will they+FOCUS rain+now   hear+will
They'll all come out now when they hear the thunder and rain

56 **Eylel-eylel**-arrene   nte elkwerr-elkwerre!
get&go away-get&go away+COMMAND you middle-middle
Pick them up half way!

12.7 Making nouns out of verbs

There are also regular ways in Kaytetye of deriving one sort of word from another, for example making a verb from a noun by adding a certain ending onto the stem of the verb, just as in English a verb like 'speak' has an equivalent noun 'speaker'.

One way of doing this is to add the ending +**wene** onto the verb stem. Some nouns, such as the bird names below, have this ending as part of their stem.

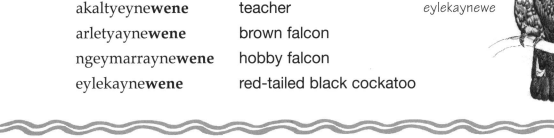

angkenke	talks
angke**wene**	one who always talks, speaker
kwathenke	drink
kwathe**wene**	drinker, drink, drinkable
alarrenke	kill, hit
alarre**wene**	killer, gun
akaltyeynenke	teach
akaltyeyne**wene**	teacher
arletyayne**wene**	brown falcon
ngeymarrayne**wene**	hobby falcon
eylekayne**wene**	red-tailed black cockatoo

eylekaynewe

Beware
This is the same ending you learnt in section 4.7, where it meant 'must', 'have to', 'let's'; however, the translation here is quite different.

Sometimes **-angkere** is added to the above forms, so instead of **angkewene** you get **angkewen-angkere** 'someone who talks all the time'. This turns a verb into a word which has the meaning of 'a person or thing who usually does the verb action, or has the verb action done to them'.

57 kwathe**wen-angkere**   drinker

pwe**wen-angkere**   a cooker (stove)

This ending can also go straight onto a noun to show that the person is characterised by this quality.

58 Kwerre nharte arrkant-**angkere**

girl   that   fun-er

That girl is a joker/fun loving

Another way to show that a person is characterised by this quality is to add +**y** onto the verb stem and then add the noun ending +**althe**, which means 'someone who is like this, or characterised by this', although only some verbs can be made into nouns in this way.

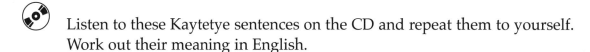

59 akenke   cry

ake**yalthe**   one who cries a lot, crybaby

60 ankeye   greedy

anke**yalthe**   greedy one

The ending +**althe** can also occur on nouns to mean someone who is like this.

61 nyerre   shy, shame

nyerr**althe**   shy person

Test your skill 12

Listen to dialogue 12 again. Write down the Kaytetye, and an English translation for it.

Listen to these Kaytetye sentences on the CD and repeat them to yourself. Work out their meaning in English.

1   Arerr-apeynterantye+ngele re arlelke aperrane+ngele.

2   Alemepe ayenge aterarrerane ntheketyarte, aleke+le atyenge atnheme-ketye.

3   Aleme atyenge aheneynenye artnwenge+le.

4   Atyewenhe elpathenke aleme angayele.

5   Nyarte atyewenhe elpatherrantye arntetye.

6   Kwenyele aylake kwere areweth-anenhe.

7   Weye atyenge etnyey-aytenye artweye+le.

8   Aynanthepe arerr-apeynterantyewethe weye+we, alewatyerre+we.

9   Ngkwarlepe eyler-apeyneyayne kwerartepe tharrkarrepe, rntwer-apeyneyayne.

10   Arrtyelere-warle aynanthe eyleyern-alpeyayne pwelekepe.

11   Angkwety-aperte arrenye atye artntweyenewethe.

Appendices

Appendix 1
Theme-based wordlist

Following is a short Kaytetye wordlist with the words grouped according to meaning rather than in alphabetical order. If you want a full alphabetical list of Kaytetye words these can be found in the *Kaytetye Wordlist,* which can be obtained from the Central Australian Dictionary Program at the Institute for Aboriginal Development. A Kaytetye to English Dictionary is also in preparation and should be available in the near future. Because this is only a wordlist, the full meanings of the following words are not reproduced here. Remember, too, that there is not always a direct correspondence between a Kaytetye word and an English word.

Edible animals

ahenenye	carpet snake
aherre	kangaroo
alewatyerre	goanna
areynenge	euro
arrepwerle	black-headed python
arwengerrpe	bush turkey
atnhelengkwe	emu
atywenpe	perentie lizard
enewaylenge	echidna
rapete	rabbit

Birds

anganke	crow
antyarlkwe	bird's nest
eylpertenye	wedge-tailed eagle
kerrkerlantye	hawk
kwarte	egg
lyerre-lyerre	wren
ngeymarre	zebra finch
paympelhe	feather, wing
thangkerne	bird

Reptiles and insects

akarntety-arntetye	gecko
amenge	fly
apmwe	snake
arreme	lice
atnyemayte	witchetty grubs

kaperle	small lizard
kalyampe	frog
ntelyapelyape	butterfly
tyewalhe	ant
wepe	spider, spider's web

Plants

alperre	leaf
arlperre	whitewood (*Atalaya hemiglauca*)
arlkerre	bush tomato (*Solanum centrale*)
arnewetye	conkerberry tree (*Carissa lanceolata*)
artetye	mulga (*Acacia aneura*)
arwele, ateye	tree, stick
athe	grass
atnkerre	coolibah tree (*Eucalyptus coolibah*)
aylpele	river red gum (*Eucalyptus camaldulensis*)
eylawe	pigweed, munyeroo (*Portulaca oleracea*)
eyleke	prickle, thorn
eylpwere	hollow tree
kartawarre	root

ngkwarle,	
maynteye	*Solanum cleistogamum*
tharrkarre	honey grevillea (*Grevillea juncifolia*)

Weather and the sky

ahepetewe	summer, hot weather
aherrke	sun
alkere	sky
arelpe	moon
arntwe	fresh water, rain
arntweng-areye	rainy season
atnkwarenge	night
kwerralye	star
lyerrmewe	winter
mataye	cloud
rarre	wind

Landforms and landscape

aherne	ground, earth, land
alpawe	plain, desert
arnerre	rockhole
artne	scrub
artnte	hill, mountain, rock, stone
elpaye	creek, river
enteye, etnteye	cave
twerrpe	sand, sandhill

Types of people

akwerrke	baby
alethange	stranger
aleyake	young woman
altye	relative, family
amarle	female, girl
arelhe	woman
artnwenge	child
artweye	man, adult male, Aboriginal person
awerre	male, boy
erlkwe	old man
eyterrtye	body, person
kwerre	girl

methethe	white woman
ngangkaye	Aboriginal doctor
ngkarte	priest
pwenge	old woman
rlwampe	boss, white man

Human relationships

alkereye, kakeye	brother (older)
yaye, arrereye	sister (older)
atyerreye	younger sibling
mpwerneye	spouse, husband's brother
atnkeleye	cross-cousin
atyeleye	female's female cross-cousin
arlweye	father
arrengkwe	mother
akeleye	father's sister, auntie
aweleye, apmarleye	mother's brother, uncle
aperleye	father's mother
arrengeye	father's father
atyewarleye, tyatye	mother's father
aytnmenheye, nyanye	mother's mother
ahenterre	father-in-law, husband's father, son's wife
anherreye	woman's daughter-in-law/mother-in-law
twaltye, mweye-mweye	man's mother-in-law, woman's son-in-law

Note

These are only a selection of Kaytetye kin terms. All of these kin terms have other possible translation equivalents. The dictionary will give more details.

Parts of the body

ahentye	throat
akantye	tail
ake	head
akwe, tyarlenye	arm, foreleg of animals
aleme	stomach, liver
alenye	tongue
anaty-anatye	heart
angketye	foot, footprint
antere	fat
areltye	lungs
arlentye	hip
arlke	body flesh
arnalke	chest
arre	mouth
arreyle	cheek
arrknge	blood
arrwete	beard
artepe	back
atnaympe	buttocks
atne	guts, faeces
atnentye	front of neck
aylpatye	breast
elhe	nose
eltye	hand
enngerre	face
erlwe	eye
errpe	knee
errtywerne	tooth
etntye, entye	hair, fur
eylepere	thigh
eylpe	ear
kwenpe	calf
lhenpe	armpit
ngkarralye	ribs
ngkwerne	bone
perrtnye	skin
pwetyerre	marrow
rlwetnperre	forehead
tyelep-etyelepe	navel

Bodily states and reactions

ampwarrenke	die
ampweyampe	thin
arapeke	weak, crippled
arlatnarrerane	cry
arntetye	sick
arrkante	laugh, fun
atnke	alive
atnkwe	asleep
atyewe	awake
kwetnaye	tired
ngayele	hungry
ntyerrele	thirsty

Social and emotional states

ahenge	angry
ahentye anteyane	want, feel like
akaltye	wise, knowledgable
akerleyte	calm, relaxed
akngwe	mad, stupid
alhewere	confident
althere	lonely, homesick
altyarrerane	happy
amperrnge	sad, unhappy
arrawerrnge	worry, yearn
arwelthe	jealous
atere	scared
athamarrerane	worried
ekwele	sulking, sulky
etarrerane	ponder, think, feel
eytenyarrerane	fall in love
nyerre	shame, shy
tyake	clever
tywekere, atnkwanenye	dislike

Religion and the supernatural

Altyerre	Aboriginal Law, Dreaming
arrentye	monster, bad spirit
arreytne	song
awelye	women's corroboree
aylerantye	sing
erntweyane	(women) dance
etnherrantye	(men) dance
etnwenge	person's spirit
lhangkele	sacred
ltharte	corroboree

Tools and weapons

akwerre	coolamon
amerre	woomera, spear thrower
arekenye	wooden scoop, shovel
arne	water vessel
arrantye	skin water bag
atneme	yamstick, crowbar
atnkere	spinifex wax, chisel
elepe	axe, tomahawk
errtyarte	spear
karlarte	shield
kayle	boomerang
kwetere	nulla nulla
makerte	gun
nkwartetye	stone knife
rape	plastic bottle
yakwethe	bag, sack

Camp and fire

aleke	dog
apmere	place, home, camp
apmerrke	hot ashes or earth
elpalhe	smoke
elye	shelter, shade
rlwakeyte	windbreak
ware	fire, firewood
warle, warleye	house, building

Eating, drinking and cooking

alepetyenke	taste, try
ampenke	heat, boil, burn, ripen
arletye	raw, uncooked, unripe
atnwenthe, weye	meat
awentyenke	lick, kiss
aynenke	eat
elpateynenke	singe
kayte	grub
kwathenke	drink
ngkwarle	sweet, sweet food
nteyngke	firm, cooked, ripe
pweke	rotten
pwenke	bake, roast, cook
rlwene, enye	vegetable food, bread
yerrampe, errampe	honey ant

Thought, speech and perception

ahelaytnenke	yell out, call
akaltyarrenke	learn
akaltyeynterantye	teach
alwengayenke	ask
angkenke	talk, say something
arenke	see, look
arntwenke	tell, say
elpathenke	hear, understand
enthwenke	search, look for
etarrenke	think
eytntenke	smell something

Motion

alpenke	go back
anamarrenke	move (self) away
apenke	go
apenkerne	come
apeyaytenke	arrive
artnangeynenke	move (something)
artnpenke	run
atneyaytenke	get up
atnthenke	fall
atntheyaytenke	climb
atnywerrane	enter, go in
elpere	quickly
eynteralwenke	follow
kartarte	slowly
kengkarrenke	sneak up on
lwemanenke	come out

Rest

altyanenke	bend over, crouch
anenke	stay, sit
atnenke	stand
aweparenke	wait
enwenke	lie

Getting, taking, giving, holding, putting

akarreynenke	gather something up
alpereynenke	take back
apereynenke	carry, take
arntarrtyenke	grab, snatch
arrenke	put down
arrtyenke	have, hold
eletnhenke	throw away
ethwenke	send
etnyenke	give
eylenke	get, pick up

Effects (physical impact)

alarrenke	hit, punch, kill
ampenke	burn
angenke	dig, scoop
apmenke	dig (with a tool)
arntenke	break
arrkweynenke	slice, cut meat
artenke	chop
atnhenke	bite
aytnenke	spear, pierce, sew
errkenke	scratch something
errkwenke	wash
ertntwenke	push
etnpenke	cover
eyenke	grind
eylpakenke	pull out
mpwarenke	fix, make, do
perrtyenke	tie up
rntwenke	cut, break off

Physical properties

ahene	good
akarntenge	short
akelye	little
alkenhe	big
ametye	blunt
amper-ampere	crooked
apal-apale	wrongly, without thinking
arlkarle	cold
arlkeny-arlkenye	stripy
arlpawe	wide
arltere	white
arreylpe	sharp
arrkwentye	a few
atnawerre	straight, right, proper
awatnkenye	old
awenyerre	one, only
aynterrke	dry
elpertarre	hard
epwane	narrow
erntetyeng-erntetyenge	spotted
errpatye	bad, spoilt
errpwerle	black
etnkwelthe	long, tall
rlengkenye	recently, new

Evaluation

makwele	many
malangke	nice, beautiful

Quantity and size

atherre	two, a pair
rarre	true, genuine
rlengkenye	new
warenpe	hot

Location

akngerrake	east
altemarle	west
antengetheye	behind
anthenayne	on the other side of
arlenge	far, long way
arrere	near, close
arrerentye	on this side of, close by
arrwekele	in front of, ahead
atnteyerre	south
ayerrere	north
elkwerre	in between, middle
errwele	high, above
kwene	under, inside

Time

aherrke	day, sun
alele	soon, wait
apertame	again
arrertame	permanent
atnkwarengele	at night, tonight
atwerrpe	late afternoon
awatnke	long ago
eyntemaperte	always
kwenyele	yesterday
kngwere-kngwere	another time, sometime
ngwenge	tomorrow
ngwetyanpe	in the morning, this morning
nthakentye- ngwere?	how long for? how many days/times/nights?
rlengke	now, today
tneyele	later

Appendix 2
Kaytetye–English wordlist

ahelaytnenke	call, yell out
ahene	good
ahenenye	carpet snake
ahenge	angry
ahenterre	father-in-law, son's wife, husband's father
ahentye	throat
ahepetewe	summer, hot weather
aherne	land, ground, earth
aherre	kangaroo
aherrke	day, sun
akaltyarrenke	learn
akaltye	wise, knowledgeable
akaltyeynterantye	teach
akantye	tail
akarntenge	short
akarntety-arntetye	gecko
akarreynenke	gather something up
ake	head
akeleye	aunty, father's sister
akelye	little
akerleyte	calm, relaxed
akngerrake	east
akngwe	mad, stupid
akwe	arm, foreleg of animals
akwerre	coolamon, baby
alarrenke	hit, kill, punch
aleke	dog
alele	soon, wait
aleme	stomach, liver
alenye	tongue
alepetyenke	taste, try
alethange	stranger
alewatyerre	goanna
aleyake	young woman
alhewere	confident
alkenhe	big
alkere	sky
alkereye	brother (older)
alkwarreye	bush banana
alpawe	desert, plain
alpenke	go back
alpereynenke	take back
alperre	leaf

altemarle	west
althere	homesick, lonely
altyanenke	bend over, crouch
altyarrerane	happy
altye	family, relative
altyeleye	female's female cousin
Altyerre	Aboriginal Law, Dreaming
alwengayenke	ask
amarle	female, girl
amelh-amelhe	brown
amenge	fly
amerre	woomera, spear thrower
ametye	blunt
ampenke	heat, burn, boil, ripen
amper-ampere	crooked
amperrnge	unhappy, sad
ampwarrenke	die
ampweyampe	thin
anamarrenke	move (self) away
anaty-anatye	heart
anenke	sit, stay
anganke	crow
angenke	dig, scoop
angkenke	talk, say something
angketye	foot, footprint
anherreye	woman's daughter-in-law /mother-in-law
antengetheye	behind
antere	fat
anthenayne	on the other side of
antyarlkwe	bird's nest
antywe	humpy, nest
apal-apale	wrongly, without thinking
aparle	dogwood seeds
apenke	go
apenkerne	come
apereynenke	take, carry
aperleye	father's mother
apertame	again
apeyaytenke	arrive
apmarleye	uncle, mother's brother
apmenke	dig (with a tool)
apmere	place, camp, home

apmerrke	hot ashes or earth
apmwe	snake
arapeke	weak, crippled
arekenye	shovel, wooden scoop
arelhe	woman
arelpe	moon
areltye	lungs
arenke	look, see
areynenge	euro
arlatnarrerane	cry
arlenge	far, long way
arlentye	hip
arletye	raw, uncooked, unripe
arlkarle	cold
arlke	body flesh
arlkeny-arlkenye	stripy
arlkerre	*Solanum centrale* (bush tomato)
arlpawe	wide
arlperre	*Atalaya hemiglauca* (whitewood)
arltere	white
arlweye	father
arnalke	chest
arne	water vessel
arnerre	rockhole
arnewetye	*Carissa lanceolata* (conkerberry tree)
arntarrtyenke	grab, snatch
arntenke	break
arntetye	sick
arntwe	rain, fresh water
arntweng-areye	rainy season
arntwenke	say, tell
arrangkere	want, feel like
arrantye	water bag (skin)
arrawarrnge	worry, yearn
arre	mouth
arreme	lice
arrengeye	father's father
arrengkwe	mother
arrenke	put down
arrentye	monster, bad spirit
arrepwerle	black-headed python
arrere	close, near
arrerentye	close by, on this side of
arrereye	sister (older)
arrertame	permanent
arreyle	cheek

arreylpe	sharp
arreytne	song
arrkante	fun, laugh
arrkare	(his/her, your) spouse
arrknge	blood
arrkwentye	(a) few
arrkweynenke	slice, cut meat
arrtyenke	have, hold
arrwekele	in front of, ahead
arrwete	beard
artenke	chop
artepe	back
artetye	*Acacia aneura* (mulga)
artnangeynenke	move (something)
artne	scrub
artnpenke	run
artnte	hill, mountain, rock, stone
artnwenge	child
artweye	Aboriginal person, man, adult male
arwele	stick, tree
arwelthe	jealous
arwengerrpe	bush turkey
atere	scared
ateye	stick, tree
athamarrerane	worried
athe	grass
atherre, atherrarte	two
atnawerre	straight, right, proper
atnaympe	buttocks
atne	faeces, guts
atneme	yamstick, crowbar
atnenke	stand
atnentye	front of neck
atneyaytenke	get up
atnhelengkwe	emu
atnhenke	bite
atnke	alive
atnkeleye	cross-cousin
atnkere	spinifex wax, chisel
atnkerre	*Eucalyptus coolibah* (coolibah tree)
atnkwanenye	dislike
atnkwarenge	night
atnkwarengele	at night, tonight
atnkwe	asleep
atnteyerre	south
atnthenke	fall
atntheyaytenke	climb

atnwenthe	meat	erlwakeyte	windbreak
atnyemayte	witchetty grub	erlwe	eye
atnywerrane	enter	erntetyeng-erntetyenge	spotted
atnywerrane	go in		
atwerrpe	late afternoon	erntweyane	dance (women)
atyerreye	sibling (younger)	errampe	honey ant
atyewarleye	mother's father	errkenke	scratch something
atyewe	awake	errkwenke	wash
atynemayte	witchetty grubs	errpatye	bad, spoilt
atywenpe	perentie lizard	errpe	knee
awankenye	old	errpwerle	black
awatnke	long ago	errtyarte	spear
aweleye	uncle, mother's brother	errtywerne	tooth
awelye	women's corroboree	errwele	high, above
awentyenke	lick, kiss	ertntwenke	push
awenyerre	one, only	etarrenke	think
aweparrenke	wait	etarrerane	think, feel, ponder
awerre	boy, male	ethwenke	send
ayerrere	north	etnherrantye	dance (men)
aylerantye	sing	etnkwelthe	long, tall
aylpatye	breast, milk	etnpenke	cover
aylpele	*Eucalyptus camaldulensis* (river red gum)	etntye	hair, fur
		etnwenge	person's spirit
aynenke	eat	etnyenke	give
aynterrke	dry	etwerrpe	sand, sandhill
aytnenke	spear, pierce, sew	eyenke	grind
aytnmenheye	mother's mother	eylawe	*Portulaca oleracea* (pigweed, munyeroo)
ekwele	sulking, sulky		
elepe	axe, tomahawk	eyleke	thorn, prickle
eletnhenke	throw away	eylenke	get, pick up
elhe	nose	eylepere	thigh
elkwerre	middle, in between	eylpakenke	pull out
elpalhe	smoke	eylperalkere	sugarbag
elpateynenke	singe	eylpertenye	wedge-tailed eagle
elpathenke	hear, understand	eylpweralke	sugarbag
elpaye	creek, river	eylpwere	hollow tree
elpere	quickly	eyntemarte, eyntemaperte	always
elpertarre	hard		
eltye	hand	eynteralwenke	follow
elye	shade, shelter	eytenyarrerane	fall in love
enewaylenge	echidna	eyterrtye	person, body
engwere-engwere	another time, sometime	eytntenke	smell something
enngerre	face	kakeye	brother (older)
enteye	cave	kalyampe	frog
enthwenke	search, look for	kaperle	small lizard
enwenke	lie	karlarte	shield
enye	bread, vegetable food	kartarte	slowly
epwane	narrow	kartawarre	root
erlkwe	old man	kayle	boomerang

kayte	grub	nyanye	mother's mother
kengkarrenke	sneak up on	nyerre	shame, shy
kerrkerlantye	hawk	pakete	bucket
kwarte	egg	paympelhe	feather, wing
kwathenke	drink	perrtnye	skin
kwene	inside, under	perrtyenke	tie up
kwenpe	calf	pweke	rotten
kwenyele	yesterday	pwenge	old woman
kwerre	girl	pwenke	bake, cook, roast
kwerralye	star	pwetyerre	marrow
kwetere	nulla nulla	rape	plastic bottle
kwetnaye	tired	rapete	rabbit
lhangkele	sacred	rarre	genuine, true
lhenpe	armpit	rarre	wind
ltharte	corroboree	rlengke	now, today
lwampe	boss, white man	rlengkenye	new, recently
lwemanenke	come out	rlwene	bread, vegetable food
lyerre-lyerre	wren	rlwetnperre	forehead
lyerrmewe	winter	rntwenke	break off, cut
makerte	gun	thangkerne	bird
makwele	many	tharrkarre	*Grevillea juncifolia*
malangke	beautiful, nice		(honey grevillea)
mataye	cloud	tneyele	later
maynteye	*Solanum cleistogamum*	twaltye	man's mother-in-law,
methethe	white woman		woman's son-in-law
mpwarenke	make, fix, do	tyake	clever
mpwerneye	spouse, husband's	tyarlenye	arm, foreleg of animals
	brother	tyatye	mother's father
mwernarte	this side	tyelepetyelepe	navel
mweye-mweye	man's mother-in-law,	tyewalhe	ant
	woman's son-in-law	tywekere	dislike
ngangkaye	Aboriginal doctor	wampere	possum
ngayele	hungry	ware	fire, firewood
ngeymarre	zebra finch	warenpe	hot
ngkarralye	ribs	warle, warleye	building, house
ngkarte	priest	wepe	spider, spider's web
ngkertarrenke	naughty	weye	meat
ngkwarle	*Solanum cleistogamum*	yakwethe	bag, sack
ngkwarle	sweet, sweet food	yathenke	pour
ngkwerne	bone	yaye	sister (older)
ngwenge	tomorrow	yerrampe	honey ant
ngwetyanpe	this morning, in the morning		
nkwartetye	stone knife		
ntelyapelyape	butterfly		
nteyngke	firm, ripe, cooked		
nthakentye-ngwere?	how long for? how many days/times/nights?		
ntyerrele	thirsty		

Appendix 3
English–Kaytetye wordlist

Aboriginal doctor	ngangkaye	boil	ampenke
Aboriginal Law	Altyerre	bone	ngkwerne
Aboriginal person	artweye	boomerang	kayle
above	errwele	boss	lwampe
Acacia aneura (mulga)	artetye	boy	awerre
adult male	artweye	bread	rlwene, enye
afternoon (late)	atwerrpe	break	arntenke
again	apertame	break off	rntwenke
ahead	arrwekele	breast	aylpatye
alive	atnke	brother (older)	alkereye, kakeye
always	eyntemaperte	brown	amelh-amelhe
angry	ahenge	building	warle, warleye
another time	engwere-engwere	burn	ampenke
ant	tyewalhe	bush tomato (*Solanum*	arlkerre
arm	akwe, tyarlenye	centrale)	
armpit	lhenpe	bush turkey	arwengerrpe
arrive	apeyaytenke	butterfly	ntelyapelyape
ask	alwengayenke	buttocks	atnaympe
asleep	atnkwe	calf	kwenpe
at night	atnkwarengele	call	ahelaytnenke
Atalaya hemiglauca	arlperre	calm	akerleyte
(whitewood)		camp	apmere
auntie	akeleye	*Carissa lanceolata*	arnewetye
awake	atyewe	(conkerberry tree)	
axe	elepe	carpet snake	ahenenye
baby	akwerrke	carry	apereynenke
back	artepe	cave	enteye
bad	errpatye	cheek	arreyle
bad spirit	arrentye	chest	arnalke
bag	yakwethe	child	artnwenge
bake	pwenke	chisel	atnkere
beard	arrwete	chop	artenke
beautiful	malangke	clever	tyake
behind	antengetheye	climb	atntheyaytenke
bend over	altyanenke	close	arrere
big	alkenhe	close by	arrerentye
bird	thangkerne	cloud	mataye
bird's nest	antyarlkwe, antywe	cold	arlkarle
bite	atnhenke	come	apenkerne
black	errpwerle	come out	lwemanenke
black-headed python	arrepwerle	confident	alhewere
blood	arrknge	conkerberry tree	arnewetye
blunt	ametye	(*Carissa lanceolata*)	
body	eyterrtye	cook	pwenke
body flesh	arlke	cooked	nteyngke

coolamon	akwerre	far	arlenge
coolibah tree	atnkerre	fat	antere
(*Eucalyptus coolibah*)		father	arlweye
corroboree	ltharte	father's father	arrengeye
cousin, female's female	altyeleye	father's mother	aperleye
cousin, male	atnkeleye	father's sister	akeleye
cover	etnpenke	father-in-law	ahenterre
creek	elpaye	feather	paympelhe
crippled	arapeke	feel	etarrerane
crooked	amper-ampere	feel like (want)	arrangkere
crouch	altyanenke	female	amarle
crow	anganke	(a) few	arrkwentye
crowbar	atneme	fire	ware
cry	arlatnarrerane	firewood	ware
cut	rntwenke	firm	nteyngke
cut meat	arrkweynenke	fix	mpwarenke
dance (men)	etnherrantye	fly	amenge
dance (women)	erntweyane	follow	eynteralwenke
day	aherrke	foot	angketye
desert	alpawe	footprint	angketye
die	ampwarrenke	forehead	rlwetnperre
dig	angenke	foreleg of animals	akwe, tyarlenye
dig (with a tool)	apmenke	fresh water	arntwe
dislike	tywekere, atnkwanenye	frog	kelyampe
		front of neck	atnentye
do	mpwarenke	fun	arrkante
dog	aleke	fur	etntye
Dreaming	Altyerre	gather something up	akarreynenke
drink	kwathenke	gecko	akarntety-arntetye
dry	aynterrke	genuine	rarre
ear	eylpe	get	eylenke
earth	aherne	get up	atneyaytenke
east	akngerrake	girl	amarle. kwerre
eat	aynenke	give	etnyenke
echidna	enewaylenge	go	apenke
egg	kwarte	go back	alpenke
emu	atnhelengkwe	go in	atnywerrane
enter	atnywerrane	goanna	alewatyerre
Eucalyptus camaldu-	aylpele	good	ahene
lensis (river red gum)		grab	arntarrtyenke
Eucalyptus coolibah	atnkerre	grass	athe
(coolibah tree)		*Grevillea juncifolia*	tharrkarre
euro	areynenge	(honey grevillea)	
eye	erlwe	grind	eyenke
face	enngerre	ground	aherne
faeces	atne	grub	kayte
fall	atnthenke	gun	makerte
fall in love	eytenyarrerane	guts	atne
family	altye	hair	etntye

hand	eltye	lie	enwenke
happy	altyarrerane	little	akelye
hard	elpertarre	liver	aleme
have	arrtyenke	lonely	althere
hawk	kerrkerlantye	long	etnkwelthe
head	ake	long ago	awatnke
hear	elpathenke	long way	arlenge
heart	anaty-anatye	look	arenke
heat	ampenke	look for	enthwenke
high	errwele	long	etnkwelthe
hill	artnte	lungs	areltye
hip	arlentye	mad	akngwe
hit	alarrenke	make	mpwarenke
hold	arrtyenke	male	awerre
hollow tree	eylpwere	man	artweye
home	apmere	man's mother-in-law	twaltye,
homesick	althere		mweye-mweye
honey ant	yerrampe, errampe	many	makwele
honey grevillea	tharrkarre	marrow	pwetyerre
(*Grevillea juncifolia*)		meat	atnwenthe, weye
hot	warenpe	middle	elkwerre
hot ashes or earth	apmerrke	monster	arrentye
hot weather	ahepetewe	moon	arelpe
house	warle, warleye	mother	arrengkwe
how long for?	nthakentye-ngwere?	mother's brother	aweleye, apmarleye
how many days/times/	nthakentye-ngwere?	mother's father	atyewarleye, tyatye
nights?		mother's mother	aytnmenheye,
humpy	antywe		nyanye
hungry	ngayele	mountain	artnte
husband's brother	mpwerneye	mouth	arre
husband's father	ahenterre	move (self) away	anamarrenke
in between	elkwerre	move (something)	artnangeynenke
in front of	arrwekele	mulga (*Acacia aneura*)	artetye
in the morning	ngwetyanpe	munyeroo (*Portulaca*	eylawe
inside	kwene	*oleracea*)	
jealous	arwelthe	narrow	epwane
kangaroo	aherre	navel	tyelepetyelepe
kill	alarrenke	near	arrere
kiss	awentyenke	new	rlengkenye
knee	errpe	nest	antyarlkwe, antywe
knowledgeable	akaltye	nice	malangke
land	aherne	night	atnkwarenge
late afternoon	atwerrpe	north	ayerrere
later	tneyele	nose	elhe
laugh	arrkante	now	rlengke
leaf	alperre	nulla nulla	kwetere
learn	akaltyarrenke	old	awankenye
lice	arreme	old man	erlkwe
lick	awentyenke	old woman	pwenge

on the other side of	anthenayne	sad	amperrnge
on this side of	arrerentye	sand, sandhill	etwerrpe
one	awenyerre	say	arntwenke
only	awenyerre	say something	angkenke
(a) pair	therre	scared	atere
perentie lizard	atywenpe	(to) scoop	angenke
permanent	arrertame	scoop (wooden)	arekenye
person	eyterrtye	scratch something	errkenke
person's spirit	etnwenge	scrub	artne
pick up	eylenke	search	enthwenke
pierce	aytnenke	see	arenke
pigweed (*Portulaca oleracea*)	eylawe	send	ethwenke
		sew	aytnenke
place	apmere	shade	elye
plain	alpawe	shame	nyerre
plastic bottle	rape	sharp	arreylpe
ponder	etarrerane	shelter	elye
Portulaca oleracea (pigweed, munyeroo)	eylawe	shield	karlarte
		short	akarntenge
prickle	eyleke	shovel	arekenye
priest	ngkarte	shy	nyerre
proper	atnawerre	sibling (younger)	atyerreye
pull out	eylpakenke	sick	arntetye
punch	alarrenke	sing	aylerantye
push	ertntwenke	singe	elpateynenke
put down	arrenke	sister (older)	yaye, arrereye
quickly	elpere	sit	anenke
rabbit	rapete	skin	perrtnye
rain	arntwe	sky	alkere
rainy season	arntweng-areye	slice	arrkweynenke
raw	arletye	slowly	kartarte
recently	rlengkenye	small lizard	kaperle
relative	altye	smell something	eytntenke
relaxed	akerleyte	smoke	elpalhe
ribs	ngkarralye	snake	apmwe
right	atnawerre	snatch	arntarrtyenke
ripe	nteyngke	sneak up on	kengkarrenke
ripen	ampenke	*Solanum centrale* (bush tomato)	arlkerre
river	elpaye		
river red gum (*Eucalyptus camaldulensis*)	aylpele	*Solanum cleistogamum*	ngkwarle, maynteye
		sometime	engwere-engwere
roast	pwenke	son's wife	ahenterre
rock	artnte	song	arreytne
rockhole	arnerre	soon	alele
root	kartawarre	south	atnteyerre
rotten	pweke	spear	errtyarte, aytnenke
run	artnpenke	spear thrower	amerre
sack	yakwethe	spider,	wepe
sacred	lhangkele	spider's web	

spinifex wax	atnkere	two	therre
spoilt	errpatye	uncle	aweleye, apmarleye
spotted	erntetyeng-erntetyenge	uncooked	arletye
		under	kwene
spouse	mpwerneye	understand	elpathenke
stand	atnenke	unhappy	amperrnge
star	kwerralye	unripe	arletye
stay	anenke	vegetable food	rlwene, enye
stick	arwele, ateye	wait	aweparrenke, alele
stomach	aleme	want	arrangkere
stone	artnte	wash	errkwenke
stone knife	nkwartetye	water bag (skin)	arrantye
straight	atnawerre	water vessel	arne
stranger	alethange	weak	arapeke
stripy	arlkeny-arlkenye	wedge-tailed eagle	eylpertenye
stupid	akngwe	west	altemarle
sugarbag	eylperalkere, eylpweralke	white	arltere
		white man	lwampe
sulking, sulky	ekwele	white woman	methethe
summer	ahepetewe	whitewood (*Atalaya hemiglauca*)	arlperre
sun	aherrke		
sweet, sweet food	ngkwarle	wide	arlpawe
tail	akantye	wind	rarre
take	apereynenke	windbreak	erlwakeyte
take back	alpereynenke	wing	paympelhe
talk	angkenke	winter	lyerrmewe
tall	etnkwelthe	wise	akaltye
taste	alepetyenke	witchetty grubs	atynemayte
teach	akaltyeynterantye	woman	arelhe
tell	arntwenke	woman's daughter-in-law /mother-in-law	anherreye
thigh	eylepere		
thin	ampweyampe	woman's son-in-law	twaltye, mweye-mweye
think	etarrerane, etarrenke		
thirsty	ntyerrele	women's corroboree	awelye
this morning	ngwetyanpe	woomera	amerre
thorn	eyleke	worried	athamarrerane
throat	ahentye	worry	arrawarrnge
throw away	eletnhenke	wren	lyerre-lyerre
tie up	perrtyenke	wrongly, without thinking	apalapale
tired	kwetnaye	yamstick	atneme
today	rlengke	yearn	arrawarrnge
tomahawk	elepe	yell out	ahelaytnenke
tomorrow	ngwenge	yesterday	kwenyele
tongue	alenye	young woman	aleyake
tonight	atnkwarengele	zebra finch	ngeymarre
tooth	errtywerne		
tree	arwele, ateye		
true	rarre		
try	alepetyenke		

Appendix 4
Summary of endings shown in this learner's guide

Note

A + sign at the end of one of these endings means that it must be followed by another ending.

Most of these endings must go on either verbs or nouns. If the 'goes on...' column is blank, it means the ending can go on both.

ending	goes on...	approximate meaning	abbrev- iation	page ref.
-akake	noun	having	having	91
+ake(rre)	pronoun	same patrimoiety opposite generation		123
+akerre	noun	around, in the vicinity of	around	101
+althe	noun	describes someone who has that quality		147
-amerne	noun	plural, many	PLURAL	43
-anenhe	verb	nearly, tried to	nearly	139
-anenye	noun	not having	without	67
+ange		forms question	UNCERTAIN	102
-angene	noun	side	side	142
+angke(rre)	noun	same patrimoiety same generation		123
-angkere	verb	makes a nominal, goes after +wene	er	147
-angkerrenye	noun	so that, in order to	so that	131
-angkwerre	noun	by way of, via	through	34
+anthe(rre)	noun	opposite patrimoiety		123
-apaperte		only, exclusively	only	99
+apartentye	noun	pretend, fake, not real	sort of	115
-apeke		perhaps, might	might	115
-apenye	noun	similarity	like	90
-apertame		again, as well, more	again	93
-aperte		just, still	just	99
-arenge	noun	belongs to	's	96
-arenye	noun	from (origin), association	ORIGIN	57
+arle	noun	towards, to, at	to	48
+arle		(RELATIVISER) that, which, who	that	120
+arre+	noun	become something	become	133
+arre		(RELATIVISER) that, which, who	that	120
-arrpanteye	noun	pretend, fake, not real	sort of	115
+arte	noun	DEMONSTRATIVE (e.g. that, this)	DEM	81
-artetye	noun	as far as, up to	as far as	132
-artweye	noun	owner, close association	ASSOC	97
-athathe	noun	until	until	132
-athathe	verb	until	until	110
-atheke	noun	towards, to	towards	140

ending	goes on…	approximate meaning	abbrev-iation	page ref.
-athene	noun	mistaken belief	MISTAKE	114
+awe		(EXCLAMATION) hey!	hey	33
+aye!		(EXCLAMATION) hey!	hey	33
+aye	noun	(RELATIVISER) that, which, who	that	120
+ayethe	noun	facing	facing	141
+ayle+	verb	make into something	make	134
-aytenge	noun	so that, in order to	so that	131
-aytenye	noun	so that, in order to	so that	131
-aytenye	noun	shows more of that quality	INTENSIFIER	131
-ee		keeps on going (shows that an action happens for a long time)	CONTINUE	83
+eyne+	verb	make into something	make	134
-eynenge	noun	(PLURAL) all, group of	lots	43
-kape	noun	and, as well as	and	85
-ketye	noun	because (bad consequence)	fear of	106
-ketye	verb	in case, lest, fear of	in case	107
kwe+	kin noun	his, her or their relation	his/her	72
+l-arlenge	noun	together, with	with	129
+l-alpe+	verb	do action and return	& return	144
+l-arre+	verb	doing action all the way along		145
+l-ayte+	verb	do action and go	& go	144
+le	noun	DOER, actor in a sentence	DOER	60
+le	noun	INSTRUMENT	with	79
+le	noun	location	at, in, on	78
+lke		then, next, now	now	58
+lke-rtame		in turn, after that	next	58
+lpe+	verb	happens on the way		145
+me	verb	could, can, might	CAN	115
+mere	verb	could, can, might	CAN	115
+ne	verb	command	COMMAND	62
+ng-anenye	verb	(NEGATIVE) can't, don't	not	68
-ngareye	noun	during, while, at the time when	during	111
+ngarle	verb	action done by a different actor	D/A	117
+nge	noun	actor in a sentence	DOER	60
+nge	noun	INSTRUMENT	with	79
+nge	noun	location	at, in, on	78
+ngele	verb	one action happens with another	S/A	116
+nge-penhe	verb	after having done	after	119
-ngerne	verb	this way	this way	36
+nge-wanenye	verb	(NEGATIVE) can't, don't	not	68
+ngewarle	verb	action done by a different actor	D/A	117
ngke+	pronoun	'your' relation	your	72
+nhe(rre)	verb	(PAST TENSE), action happened		97
-nhenge	noun	two people together	together	87
+nke	verb	PRESENT TENSE		35
+ntyele	verb	(NEGATIVE IMPERATIVE)	don't	69
+nye(rre)	verb	(PAST TENSE), action happened		97
+pe		FOCUS MARKER	FOCUS	36
-penhe	noun	after, from	after	57

ending	goes on...	approximate meaning	abbreviation	page ref.
-penhe	verb	after doing	after	119
+rewe	verb	while	while	111
+rne	verb	this way (*after motion verbs in present tense*)	this way	36
+rr-alpe+	verb	do action and return		144
+rrane	verb	shows action continues, or is repeated	ing	81
+r-ape+	verb			144
+rrantye	verb	shows action continues, or is repeated	ing	82
+rr-ayte+	verb	do action and go	& go	144
+rr-etnye+	verb	doing action all the way along		145
-rtame		emphasis	EMPH	74
-rtame		contrast	CONTRAST	74
-rteye		(UNCERTAIN) forms question	UNCERTAIN	102
-rwenge	noun	how many times something happens	times	138
-rwenge	verb	while	while	111
-therre	noun	two	two	43
-theye	noun	from	from	91
-tyampe		including, and	and	85
-wanenye	noun	not having	without	66
-warle	noun	towards, to, at	to	47
+watye	noun	(COMPARATIVE), '+er'	COMP	75
+we	noun	for, at, on, to	for	49
+wene	verb	changes verbs into nominals	+er	147
+wene	verb	should, have to, let's	MUST	63
+wenhe	pronoun	self	self	108
+wethe	verb	purpose or intent	PURP	92
+wethe-ketye	verb	happens before another action	before	110
+y-alpe+	verb	go back and do action	go back &	143
+yane	verb	shows action continues, or is repeated	ing	82
+yayne	verb	used to, would	used to	107
+y-ayte+	verb	come up and do action	it comes	142
+ye	kin noun	my relation	my	72
+ye(rre)	verb	FUTURE	will	51
+y-ene+	verb	go and do action	go&	143
+yern-alpe+	verb	come this way doing action	come doing	145
+yern-ayte+	verb	do action after getting up	after getting up	145
+yenge	pronoun	possessive marker	poss	71

Appendix 5
Table of Kaytetye pronouns

One person

	Doer form		Object form	Possessive	Reflexive
	transitive verb	intransitive verb			
First person I, me, my, mine, myself	atye	ayenge	atyenge	atyeyenge	atyewenhe
Second person you, your, yourself	nte	nge	ngkenge	ngkeyenge	ntewenhe
Third person he, she, it, her, him, it, hers, his, its, herself, himself, itself	re		kwere	kwereyenge	rewenhe

Two people: 'we two', 'us two'

	Doer form	Object form	Possessive	Reflexive
Same kinship group, same generation group	ayleme	aylewe	ayleweyenge	aylewenhe
Same kinship group, other generation group	aylake	aylewake	aylewakeyenge	aylewenhake
Different kinship group	aylanthe	aylewanthe	aylewantheyenge	aylewenhanthe

Two people: 'we two (not including you, the listener)'

	Doer form	Object form	Possessive	Reflexive
Same kinship group, same generation group	aylene	aylengke	aylengkeyenge	aylewenhengke
Same kinship group, other generation group	aylenake	aylekake	aylekakeyenge	aylewenhake
Different kinship group	aylenanthe	aylekanthe	aylekantheyenge	aylewenhanthe

More than two people: 'we', 'us mob'

	Doer form	Object form	Possessive	Reflexive
Same kinship group, same generation group	aynangke	aynewangke	aynewangkeyenge	aynewenhangke
Same kinship group, other generation group	aynake	aynewake	aynewakeyenge	aynewenhake
Different kinship group	aynanthe	aynewanthe	aynewantheyenge	aynewenhanthe

More than two people, not including the person being spoken to

	Doer form	Object form	Possessive	Reflexive
Same kinship group, same generation group	aynenangke	aynekangke	aynekangkeyenge	aynewenhangke
Same kinship group, other generation group	aynenake	aynekake	aynekakeyenge	aynewenhake
Different kinship group	aynenanthe	aynekanthe	aynekantheyenge	aynewenhanthe

You, you, yours (two people: 'you two')

	Doer form	Object form	Possessive	Reflexive
Same kinship group, same generation group	mpwele	mpwewe	mpweweyenge	mpwewenhe
Same kinship group, other generation group	mpwelake	mpwewake	mpwewakeyenge	mpwewenhake
Different kinship group	mpwelanthe	mpwewanthe	mpwewantheyenge	mpwewenhanthe

You, you, yours (more than two people: 'you mob')

	Doer form	Object form	Possessive	Reflexive
Same kinship group, same generation group	elweme	elwewe	elweweyenge	elwewenhe
Same kinship group, other generation group	elwake	elwewake	elwewakeyenge	elwewenhake
Different kinship group	elwanthe	elwewanthe	elwewantheyenge	elwewenhanthe

They, them, their, theirs (two people: 'they two, the two of them')

	Doer form	Object form	Possessive	Reflexive
Same kinship group, same generation group	errwangke	errwewangke	errwewangkeyenge	errwewenhe
Same kinship group, other generation group	errwake	errwewake	errwewakeyenge	errwewenhake
Different kinship group	errwanthe	errwewanthe	errwewantheyenge	errwewenhanthe

They, them, their, theirs (more than two people: 'they')

	Doer form	Object form	Possessive	Reflexive
Same kinship group, same generation group	atangke	atewangke	atewangkeyenge	atewenhangke
Same kinship group, other generation group	atake	atewake	atewakeyenge	atewenhake
Different kinship group	atanthe	atewanthe	atewantheyenge	atewenhanthe

Appendix 6
Answers to test your skill

Dialogue 1   *Arlelke*

Apenerne ngawe!

Nthek-angkwerre ngepe apenke?

Arlelke ayenge apenke. Ngepe apenkerne?

Alele, ayenge apenkerne.

Come here!

Where are you going?

I'm going hunting. Are you coming?

Wait, I'm coming.

1   Where is he going?
2   Where are you going?
3   Where is the man going?
4   Are you coming?
5   Is he coming?
6   Is the man coming?
7   I'm going (through the) bush (i.e. not on the road).
8   He is going via Alekarenge.
9   Are you going through Alice Springs?
10   The man went through Barrow Creek.
11   The dog is running across the camp.
12   We are going hunting for emu through the bush.
13   I'm coming (tomorrow) morning.

Dialogue 2   *Wante nyartepe?*

Wantepe nyartepe?

Nhartepe atnwenthe aherre.

Wante nyartepe?

Nhartepe ngkwarle yerrkeyerre.

Wante nyartepe?

Nhartepe rlwene anatye.

Wante nyartepe?

Nhartepe thangkerne atetherr-eynenge.

Wante nyartepe?

Nhartepe arwele atnkerr-amerne.

What's this?

That's a kangaroo.

What's this?

That's edible lerp.

What's this?

That's a yam.

What's that?

Those are zebra finches.

What's that?

That's a group of coolibah trees.

1   What is that?
2   This is a small creek.
3   What's this?

4   That is a big dog.

5   What is that?

6   This is a small stick.

7   What's this?

8   That is a big stone.

9   Two big black dogs.

10 All the small children.

11 Two women go to camp.

12 The men are going hunting for kangaroo.

atnwenthe/weye

rlwene/enye

atnwenthe/weye

nterrenge

rlwene/enye

rlwene/enye

atnwenthe/weye

ngkwarle

kayte

atnwenthe/weye

Dialogue 3   Mwanyeme

Apenerne nge!	Come here!
Nthek-angkwerre errwanthe apenke?	Where are you mob going?
Aynanthe elpaye-warle apenke.	We're going to the creek.
Wantewe?	What for?
Rlwene ngkwarle-maynteyewe.	For bush tomatoes.
Wante nhartepe?	What's that?
Mwanyemewe. Ngepe apenkerne?	For bush tomatoes. Do you want to come?
Anteyane ayenge, ngwenge arlelke apeye.	I'm staying, tomorrow I will go hunting.

1   I'm going to the creek.

2   The man is going to camp.

3   This meat is for the dog.

4   We are going for bush tomatoes.

5   I will go to the big creek.

6   The woman will go back to camp.

7   We are going to the creek for **mwanyeme**.

8   I'm pouring water into the bucket.

9   I'm grabbing frogs from the creek.
10 I saw a zebra finch in its nest.
11 I see the dog in the shade.
12 I will stay for good.
13 Yesterday afternoon we went to the creek.

apenke, apeye

apenkerne, aperrenenyeye

aynenke, ayneye

pwenke, pweye

yathenke, yatheye

rntwenke, rntweye

arrenke, arreye

Dialogue 4   *Nthekarenye ngaye?*

Apenerne ngawe!	Come here!
Nthakenharrerane nge?	What's up?
Ayenge ntyerrel-arrerane.	I'm thirsty.
Nthek-arenye nge?	Where are you from?
Ayenge Alekareng-arenye.	I'm from Alekarenge.
Aweleye atyeyenge Alekareng-arenye.	My uncle is from Alekarenge.
Ngkawelepe Kngwarraye-rtame?	Is your uncle a Kngwarraye?
Yewe-yewe.	Yes.
Atnkeleye, arntwe atyenge etnyewenawe!	Cousin, give me some water!
Me, kwathene nte.	Here, have a drink.
Ngepe nthek-arenye?	Where are you from?
Ayenge Artarr-arenye.	I'm from Artarre.
Me, alkaperte atye kwathenhe.	Here, finished.
Alkaperte?	Enough?
Yeah, alkaperte.	Yeah, fine.

1   The child hits the man.
2   The man sees the kangaroo.
3   The mother gives the child meat.
4   The dog eats meat.
5   Drink the soft drink!
6   Go to town!
7   Give me some money.
8   They will go back after work.

9   After that I'll get some water.

10 After a sleep I'll get up.

11 We will go after supper.

12 *Mwanyeme* grows around the creek.

13 My uncle is from the north.

14 I come from the south.

15 The children from the camp arrive at school.

Dialogue 5   *Petrol-wanenye*

Antethenene ngawe!	Stop!
Wantartaye?	What's up?
Petrol-wanenye.	No petrol.
Nthek-arenyarte nge?	Where are you from?
Ayenge *Barrow Creek*-arenye.	I'm from Barrow Creek.
John ntepe etelarrerantye?	Do you know John?
Yawe, nhartepe aweleye-rtame atyeyenge.	Yes, that's my uncle.
Repe atyeyenge atyerreye-rtame.	He's my younger brother.
Ngepe atyeyenge aweleye-rtame,	You're my uncle, could you get some
petrol atyenge katye eylewenawe!	petrol for me!
Artnte-wanenye, apeyakele. *Petrol*	(I've) got no money. (I) can't get petrol.
eylenge-wanenye.	
Nyarte ngkweltye akelye. *Petrol*	Here's a bit of money. Get some
atyenge katye eylene.	petrol for me?
Alkapertawe!	OK!

aleke atyeyenge

ngkarrengkwe

atnkeleye/altyeleye atyeyenge

atnwenthe kwereyenge

ngkarlweye

ake ayenge (atyeyenge)

kwawele

tyarlenye re (kwereyenge)

1   I haven't got any meat.

2   He hasn't got any money.

3   S/he hasn't got any children.

4   You haven't got a dog.

5   I've got no younger siblings.

6   He's not sick, he's healthy.
7   The child isn't drinking milk.
8   My dog won't eat.
9   The car isn't stopping, it's going straight past.
10 We will give them meat.
11 I will give them meat.
12 You two will give me meat.

Dialogue 6 *Nthekelarte ngepe anteyane?*

Nthekelarte ngepe anteyane?	Where do you live?
Ankweleyelengkwele ayenge anteyane. Ntharenyarte ayenge.	I live at Ankweleyelengkwe. I'm from there.
Ngkatyerr-amerne arrenentye ntepe arrtyerrantye?	How many younger siblings have you got? *(Literally, how many younger siblings do you hold?)*
Atherrarte.	Two.
Wante-rtame etnepe eleweyenge?	What are their names?
Andrew-tyampe Simon-tyampe. Aynanthe anteyane Ankweleyelengkwele.	Their names are Andrew and Simon. We live at Ankweleyelengkwe.

1   The dog is in the shade.
2   The girl is digging for yams with a digging stick.
3   The two men spear an emu.
4   Marrow is in the bone.
5   What are you making?
6   This man speared the other man.
7   Where do you live?
8   All the boys and girls are coming.
9   Give me ashes and tobacco.
10 The two sisters are going hunting for yams.
11 Bush food is better than white people's food.
12 That one is darker.
13 That one is dark black and this one is brown.
14 I put bush tomatoes and bush onions into the coolamon.
15 The dog is running about at night.
16 The man hit the dog with a stick.
17 My dog and I went to the shop.

Dialogue 7   *Aleme ayenge ngayele*

Akeleyaye, aleme ayenge ngayele! Rlwene atnwenthe-tyampe akake ngepe?	Auntie, I'm really hungry! Have you got any tucker and meat?
Alele aweparene nge, weye atye pwenke.	Wait a bit, I'm cooking some meat.
Wante nhartepe?	What's that?
Nyartepe weye alewatyerre.	This is goanna meat.
Nthakenhe nte pwenke?	How do you cook it?
Weye alewatyerre, apmerrke-le pwenke.	You cook goanna on the hot coals.
Nthakenhe nte eylenke?	How do you get it?
Alhwenge-theye nte eylenke.	You pull it out of a hole.
Weye nharte want-apenye?	What's the meat like?
Atnwenthe nyarte *chicken*-apenye. Me, alepetyene nte.	It's like chicken meat. Here, try some.
Mmm. Ekwe malangke, ahene mpele! Etnyewen-apertame atyenge!	Oh it tastes delicious, it's good! Give me some more!
Me, aynen-apertame nte!	Here, eat some more!

1 What's that food like?
2 Get me some food like that.
3 He goes from the camp.
4 I'm going to the creek to get water.
5 That boy has a hat.
6 The child has a dog.
7 Eat some more!
8 I want to eat some meat.
9 It's good that we talk language.
10 I'll keep eating the meat.
11 Let's go hunting.
12 We'll keep going hunting.
13 You mob go hunting again!
14 This food is really nice.
15 The dog is running from the camp.
16 You and I should sit in the shade to cool off.

Dialogue 8   *Store-warle apewethe*

Mpe! Apewene aynanthe *store*-warle
enye eylewethe.

Mame, arene nte ayenge ahentye anteyane
mwetekaye akelye nthewarte!

Apeyakele, eylentyele mpele! Kwenyele
ngkawelele wenharte ngkenge etnyenyerre.

Mame, arene nte! Mantarre arlkeny-arlkenye
nthewarte ayenge ahentye anteyane.

Ngkertarrentyele, mentye. Mantarre nharte
amarl-arenge. Nyarte-rteye?

Ayenge tywekere nthewarte! Aye,
nyarte-rteye?

Nhartepe artnte alkenhe-rtame. Artnte
akelye rlwenewe atnwenthewe-tyamp-aperte
eylewethe.

Come on! We're going to the store to
get food.

Mum, look! I want that car.

No, leave it! Yesterday your uncle gave
you one of them.

Mum, look! I really want those stripy
clothes.

Don't be naughty, leave it, they're
women's clothes. What about this one?

I don't like that one! Hey, what about
this one?

That one is too expensive. I've only
got a little bit of money to get meat
and tucker with.

1   Where do you live?
2   What place are you from?
3   The horse killed the man.
4   Yesterday I killed a possum.
5   I ate a soft yam.
6   Where did you come from yesterday?
7   Don't drink the bad water!
8   Sit down, don't run away.
9   I really want to eat some meat.
10   I really like that girl.
11   Is this the way to the store?
12   Is it OK if I go with you lot?

Nthekarlarte ngepe apenke?
Wante ntepe aynterantye?
Arrenentye ngkeyenge atyerrey-eynenge?
Wantewarte repe apenke?
Wantepenhe ngepe arntetye?
Nthekelarte ngepe anteyane?
Elewarte atanthe apenke?
Wantarte errwanthe mpwarerrantye?

Dialogue 9   *Arntety-arreme-ketye*

Nthakenharreyayne mpwelanthe?	What have you two been doing?
Eylatneyayne aylewenhanthe ahernele.	We've been playing in the dirt.
Eltye ntewenhe arene artennge! Eltye ntewenhe errkwene arntwenge.	Look at your hands, they're filthy! Wash your hands with water.
Wante-ketye?	What for?
Arntetyarreme-ketye elpere, errkweyenene ntewenhe rlwerne aynewethe-ketye.	Because you two might get sick. Quick go and wash your hands with water, then you can eat.
Alkaperte.	OK.

1   I'm hiding it from her.
2   Come here so you don't get left behind.
3   Come this way because of the fire.
4   Go quickly because of that man.
5   Go slowly because of the snake.
6   The dog ran away from the horse.
7   The man built a humpy as protection from the rain.
8   The quoll might bite you with his teeth!
9   They would light the fire and cook the meat.
10 I'm looking at myself in the mirror.
11 Those two separated.
12 They saw them first when they were unripe.

Dialogue 10   *Wantertetye?*

Ngalyerraye, apenerne nge! Pepe nyarte aylake arewethe.	Ngalyerre, come here, let's look at this book.
Nyarte-rtame atyepe arerrantye ngkwarle arlkarlarre atye kwathemere.	I can see a nice cold soft drink that I could drink!
Enewaylenge-nyarte, antere alkenhe ayneme atye wenharte artntenge artnperranenge-warle.	I can see a really fat echidna that I could eat!
Atnwenth-apertame! Pwelkantyew-athene atye arenherre, wante-rtetyange?	More meat! Hey I thought that was a dragon lizard, what sort is it?
Nhartepe apmwelye-arrpanteye.	It's a kind of bearded dragon from the north, from the coast.
*Top-end-*arenye etnepe re *frill-necked lizard*.	It's called a frill-necked lizard, it's from the top end.

1   If you kill a kangaroo can you bring me back some.

2   He went and shot what he thought was a kangaroo.

3   Let him go while he speaks.

4   He is looking around while talking.

5   I saw a roo while I was running.

6   When I saw the kangaroo I speared him.

7   I'm sitting talking.

8   While he is waiting he sits in the shade.

9   After drinking blood he ate some food.

10 You will eat the wallaby I speared.

11 I saw a galah eating grass.

12 I see a man going.

13 I hear you talking.

14 Go to the kangaroo that died.

15 I'm looking for the kangaroo that the man shot.

Dialogue 11   *Wante ntepe mpwarerrantye?*

Wante nte mpwarerrantye nhartepe?	What are you doing?
Artnweng-eynenge atye akaltyeynterantye.	I'm teaching the children.
Wantewarte atanthe akaltyarrerane?	What are they learning?
Akaltyarrerane atanthe elye mpwarewethe.	They are learning how to make a bough shed.
Artnwengeynengaye, alperr-eynenge errwanthe nthewarlarte atyenge katye arrene, atyaytenge elye mpwarewethe.	Children, put the leaves down there for me, so that I can make the shade.
Elye mpwareng-alkerepe aynanthe apewene elpayarlelke.	After we've made the bow shed we'll go to the creek.
Me.	Here.
Apewene aynanthe arrkantel-arlenge elpayarl-atheke.	Let's go to the creek now for fun.

1   What did you do yesterday?

2   I'm homesick for my country.

3   The money is being sent with the white woman.

4   He went with the mob from Murray Downs.

5   I'll go with you too.

6   The old man is sitting with the girl.

7   The woman is walking along with the old man.

8   They would bring the meat back to camp for the old men.

9   He'll put [the rest] to one side on a heap until he takes it back.

10 I'm going to work.

11 Why are you being quiet?

12 All right I am just telling about it so'they can check it with one another later.

13 Eating that sweet food made my belly feel better.

Dialogue 12 *Wantewarte artnwenge nhartepe akerrane?*

Wantewarte artnwenge nhartepe akerrane? Arntetye-apeke rewenhe elpatherrantyenke?	Why is the child crying? Does she feel sick?
Na, nyartepe artnwenge ekwele-rtame akerrane, *town*-warle apewethe akerrane nhartepe.	No, she's sulking because she can't go to town.
Wantewe-rtame *town*-warlepe apewethe?	Why does she want to go to town?
Ahentye anteyane re *shopping*-we.	She wants to go shopping.
Ayenge alantye apewethe!	I'm going anyway!
Artnweng-aye! Akerleytarrene nge. Atyengel-arlenge nge apeyaytewethe *town*-warle ayenge apewathe-anenke rlengkepe, ngwengelke ayenge apeyerre.	Daughter! Be quiet, you can come with me later, I'm going south.

1 He goes along looking when he is going hunting.

2 I feel frightened of that one; the dog might bite me.

3 My child made me feel better.

4 I feel hungry.

5 I feel sick.

6 Yesterday we tried to see him.

7 The man came up and gave me some meat.

8 We'll go looking for meat, goanna, around there.

9 We would pick the honey from the honey grevillea as we went along, breaking off the branches as we went along.

10 We were getting cattle as we came this way towards Arrtyelere.

11 Wait first, I'll go and tell them over there.

A Kaytetye song

Artweye erlkwe

by Vincent Janima

Artweye erlkwaye rlwakeytele anteyane
Artnwenge akelyeynengele alwengayerantyaye
'Nthekangkwerre nte artweye erlkwaye
apelapenke?'

The wise old man sits behind the wind break
And all the young children ask him
'Where are you heading off to now old
man?'

Artweye erlkwaye rlwakeytele anteyane
Artnwenge akelyeynengele alwengayerantyaye
'Artweye erlkwe nthekangkwerre nte
apelapenke?'

The wise old man sits behind the wind break
And all the young children ask him
'Where are you heading off to now old
man?'

Artnwenge akelyele alwengayerantyaye
'Erlkwe nthekangkwerre ntepe apenke?'
'Apmere atyeyengarle altwerlepenharle'

And the children ask him
'Where are you going old man?'
'I'm going to my country, westwards'

Artnwenge akelyeynengele alwengayer-
antyaye
'Artweye erlkwe nthekarle ntepe apenke?'
'Ayenge apelapenke apmere altemarle'

And the children ask him
'Where are you going old man?'
'I'm heading off to my country in the west'

Artweye erlkwaye rlwakeytele anteyane
Artnwenge akelyeynengele alwengayerantyaye
'Nthekangkwerrepe artweye erlkwe
apelapenke?'

The wise old man sits behind the wind break
And all the young children ask him
'Where are you heading off to old man?'

Artweye erlkwaye rlwakeytele anteyane
Artnwenge akelyeynengele alwengayerantyaye
'Artweye erlkwe nthekarle apmere altemarle
apelapenke?'

The wise old man sits behind the wind break
And all the young children ask him
'Old man, which country in the west are you
heading off to?'

Artnwenge akelyeynengele alwengayer-
antyaye
'Artweye erlkwe nthekarle ntepe apenke?'
'Ayenge alpenke apmere altemarle'

And the children ask him
'Where are you going, old man?'
'I'm going back to my country in the west'

Artnwenge akelyeynengele alwengayerantyaye
'Nthekarle artweye erlkwe?'
'Ayenge alpenke apmere atyeyengarle
altemarle'

And the children ask him
'Where, old man?'
'I'm going back to my country in the west'

Other Kaytetye resources

Books and articles

Breen G. 1996. Kaytetye Wordlist. Compiled from wordlists by Harold Koch and Ken Hale. Kaytetye Dictionary Project. Unpublished computer printout. Alice Springs: Institute for Aboriginal Development.

Central Australian Dictionaries Program, IAD and Thangkenharenge Aboriginal Corporation. 1998. Kaytetye Stories. [Has accompanying audio tapes]. A series of ten Kaytetye readers about bush foods. Yuendumu: Bilingual Resource Development Unit.

Hagan, R. & M. Rowell. 1978. *A Claim to Areas of Traditional Land by the Alyawarra and Kaititja.* Alice Springs: Central Land Council.

Kendon, A. 1988. *Sign languages of Aboriginal Australia: cultural, semiotic and communicative perspectives.* Cambridge: CUP.

Koch, G. 1993. *Kaytetye Country.* Alice Springs: IAD Press.

Koch, H. 1980. Kaititj nominal inflection: some comparative notes. In Rigsby and P. Sutton (eds), *Papers in Australian Linguistics No 13: Contributions to Australian Linguistics.* Pacific Linguistics Series A-59. Canberra: Australian National University. 259–76.

Koch, H. 1982. Kinship categories in Kaytej pronouns. In Heath et al. *Languages of Kinship in Aboriginal Australia.* 64–71.

Koch, H. 1983. Etymology and dictionary making for Australian languages (with examples from Kaytej). In P. Austin (ed.), *Papers in Australian Linguistics No. 15: Australian Aboriginal lexicography.* Pacific Linguistics Series A-66. Canberra: Australian National University. 149–73.

Koch, H. 1984. The category of 'associated motion' in Kaytej. *Language in Central Australia* 1. 23–34.

Koch, H. 1990. Do Australian Languages really have Morphemes? Issues in Kaytej Morphology. In P. Austin, R.M.W. Dixon, T. Dutton and I. White (eds), *Language and History: Essays in Honour of Luise A. Hercus.* Pacific Linguistics Series, C-116. Canberra: Australian National University. 193–208.

Koch, H. 1996. Reconstruction in morphology. In Mark Durie & Malcolm Ross (eds), *The comparative method reviewed: regularity and irregularity in language change.* New York: Oxford University Press. 218–63.

Koch, H. 1997. Pama-Nyungan reflexes in the Arandic languages. In Darrell Tryon and Michael Walsh (eds), *Boundary rider: Essays in Honour of Geoffrey O'Grady.* Pacific Linguistics Series, C-136. Canberra: Australian National University. 271–302.

Koch, H. In press. Basic vocabulary of the Arandic languages: From classification to reconstruction. In B. Alpher et al (eds), [Volume of papers on Australian linguistics]. Pacific Linguistics Series. Canberra: Australian National University.

Wafer, J. 1980. *Kaytetye Picture Vocabulary.* Alice Springs: Language Centre, Institute for Aboriginal Development.

Wafer, J. nd. *A simple sketch of the Kaytej language.* From field notes by Harold Koch. Alice Springs: Institute for Aboriginal Development.

Videos

"Barrow Creek" *Nganampa Anwernekenhe* Series. 1995. Alice Springs: CAAMA Productions.

Irrelalye. The Red Sand Goanna. 1999. Keith Skinner. SKS Productions.

Akwerteytenge. The Rainbow Serpent. 1999. Tommy Thompson & Myfany Turpin. SKS Productions.

Arrkantele 2000. A series of three videos teaching Kaytetye literacy. Alice Springs: Warlpiri Media Association.

Most of these references can be obtained from
Central Australian Dictionaries Program,
Institute for Aboriginal Development,
PO Box 2531, Alice Springs NT 0871.
Ph (08) 8951 1311.

CD track listings

CD 1